"Your Recipe for Life"

Work Forms, Affirmations & Daily Reminders included

For E-Book Readers: go to www.yourrecipe4life.com to Download the Work Forms, Affirmations & Daily Reminders.

Printed in the United States of America

ISBN 978-0-692-17696-2

www.yourrecipe4life.com

Acknowledgements

I must give credit to my father and mother for their support and their encouragement to get involved in new adventures. They taught us family relationship and our family of six did a lot of activities together including tennis, water sports, boating, camping, home renovation, car repair and engine overhauls to name a few. They seldom told us that we could not participate in a new endeavor. My mother, who is100 years old, still supports the entire extended family and our activities and get-togethers.

My beloved father and mother-in-law were instrumental in introducing us to a motivation and personal development program which expanded our life adventures and our personal development. This led my wife and I to discover a philosophy that believes in a very positive and uplifting doctrine that elevates one's success.

I give a big thank you to my wife Dale for establishing mutual goals throughout our life and for her great support and understanding over these 55 years of marriage.

The Civil Air Patrol Cadet Program presented me with marching and drill team experience, led me to an AA degree in aeronautics and to pilot training.

My participation in the US Naval Reserves enabled me to expand and use my knowledge and abilities and to visit other countries.

I wish to express my appreciation to the City of Upland California, my first city manager "Pinky" Alder, the city council persons who endorsed my development and expansion of the city's park and recreation programs. I am proud that as Director, my budget requests over seven years were always approved without cuts.

Without the assistance of those mentioned above and many others, I would not have accomplished my life desires or been able to present to you "Your Recipe for Life."

Fred

Introduction

I assume you are reading this book because you would like to enhance the life you are living and the life you dream of having. You may call this success.

If you are like me you have read many books, invested in recorded books and recorded materials, attended many workshops and college classes, traveled long distances, endured scarcity and lack, looking to better yourself and grow personally so you could have a more rewarding life. Undoubtedly these have taken a lot of time and most likely money. Each has enhanced your life if followed but were possibly short lived or produced mediocre results.

Many opportunities may have passed me by throughout my earlier life because I was not mentally prepared for them. Others passed me by because my ideas and goals were not acted upon because I did not learn about the art of goal setting until later in life. I will show you how to ensure opportunities do not pass you by.

In this book I have addressed that which has greatly enhanced my life and has helped others who have attended my workshops. Many of the ideas and outlined activities presented in my book may have been introduced to you before but you may not have been able to put them into practical use. My presentation, if followed, is a proven procedure that will bring results you desire. All I ask of you is to study these ideas until you understand them, practice the concepts that I present and follow through with your plan of action.

I would love to hear from you concerning the added success this book brought to you or to answer any questions you may have, (time permitting).

May your life proceed and manifest toward your greatest possible good.

In positive expectancy,

Fred

Table of Contents

Fred's Autobiography

I was born in Santa Monica, California. At age five I entered kindergarten for about six months. My father was discharged from the army and we moved to Ontario, California. After getting settled into our home, and now at age six, I went to register for the first grade. The principal recommended that I return to kindergarten because I was socially unprepared for first grade. I have never met another person that flunked kindergarten.

Later in life, I met a beautiful long-haired brunette who had a great influence on my life. Her name was Myrna Hughes. She was in my first-grade class. I was shy and still somewhat backward. I don't think she ever knew how much I admired her. It was at this time my life was established. I decided I would be a person pursuing excellence, growing in knowledge and abilities that others would look up to.

I built well engineered push carts (later with engines), model airplanes that flew well and home-made kites. I developed a few friends and they would come to my house to play with my creations, which helped me to build self-esteem and social skills. I also assisted my dad in remodeling our ninety-year-old two-story home. I always had a job, taking care of neighbor's yards, working at Graber Olive factory across the street and as a box boy (bagger). I drove a school bus while attending junior college.

I began playing tennis with my family at age nine. Before long and after considerable practice, I was entering tournaments and winning some. I became an assistant tennis instructor for the Ontario Recreation Department when I was fourteen. My parents gained permission for me to take my junior high school physical education class with the high school tennis team on the campus across the street. This really advanced my tennis abilities and boosted my self- esteem. I became a Varsity letterman in my freshman year, of which few others attained. I was in the Varsity Letterman Club, the German, Chorale and Rifle Clubs. By the time I became a senior, I was in the top one percent of all California tennis players within the eighteen and under division and continued playing tennis through college.

At age fifteen, I joined the Civil Air Patrol Cadet program. I was interested in flying and I wished to learn more about airplanes and search and rescue operations. I was chosen to be on the marching and precision drill team. We entered a national drill team competition and came in third place. What a boost in self-confidence. Being in an Air Force uniform gave me pride.

Now back to my high school days. In my senior year, I joined the Naval Air Reserves. I became a flight crew member in a bomber squadron. I now got to fly one weekend per month.

Upon graduating from high school and during that summer, I attended boot camp. Due to my marching and drill team experience, I was chosen to be the recruit company commander and was in charge of my company of eighty men. What a great experience and I was very proud of this accomplishment.

I entered the Aeronautics program (Aircraft Maintenance) at the local junior college, a five-semester course. I was president of the Aeronautics Club three out of the five semesters. The college offered a pilot training program and I received my pilot's license. I was president of the Flying Club for two semesters. Upon graduating with an associate art degree in aeronautics, I passed the federal power plant and airframe exams, qualifying me as an aircraft mechanic.

One night at our junior college football game, my brother George and I announced an after-game party at our house. Approximately eighty showed up to dance and socialize in our upstairs rooms. We later had a patio party with a band and had close to one hundred and fifty attendees.

We met Dave Aerni who knew the band that played at our patio party. We offered to promote their band and we became the managers of "The Tornadoes", and "Aertaun Enterprises" was born (Aerni/Taunton). We booked them every Friday night within the Inland Empire. We soon recorded "Bustin Surfboards" followed by two more hit recordings. The releases were on our own record label Aertaun Records. We soon needed a national distributing company to keep up with the orders and we chose Jay Gee Record and their affiliates.

The surf sounds and the stomp (a dance style) had hit the West coast with Dick Dale and the Del Tones leading the way. Aertaun Enterprises was renting the Ontario National Guard Armory to conduct a Saturday dance once a month. We averaged around eight hundred attendees per night. We hired "The Beach Boys," who also performed the surf/beach sounds, to play on a Saturday night. They performed two Saturdays and soon became so popular, they were unavailable for our dances because they were traveling. Our Tornadoes played at many Saturday dances also. Dick Dale and The Detones, already well known, performed for us also. It is a great feeling of accomplishment, to look back to the days that we helped establish the early sixties music. I attended San Jose State College for one year and received a teaching credential, while still involved with Aertaun Enterprises. At the age of twenty-one, I returned to Ontario, California and was hired by the same school district that I had graduated from.

I taught for one semester and then left for my two-year active duty obligation. My orders were to report to the USS Ticonderoga, an attack air craft carrier. Upon reporting to duty, I was placed in charge of maintaining the ship's air craft support equipment. I was only an airman but soon advanced to petty officer third class. My job included keeping the equipment in operation with minimum down time, keeping costs down and keeping the maintenance records on all equipment. I received top scores during the many inspections and evaluations.

Due to my excellent performance, I was also placed in charge of maintaining the damage control equipment of our division's spaces and the air group spaces. My commanding officer, upon discovering that I was a teacher and one of the subjects I taught was driver education, assigned me as the ship's driver licensing petty officer. He also assigned me to help those in our division who were taking correspondence courses. To say the least, I was busy, but felt honored at the same time.

Upon receiving an honorable discharge, and status as a war veteran, I resumed my teaching career, teaching driver education and tennis coach for a total of seven years. I enjoyed teaching and was popular and enjoyed supporting each of my student's personal growth.

While teaching, I continued my education at Cal State L.A. completing my Bachelor of Arts Degree and attended seminars, workshops and reading books on personal development and motivation. I applied to, and was accepted by Success Motivation Institute, an international firm, for whom I conducted seminars and workshops for companies, a college and for individuals.

About a year later the city of Upland, California advertised for a part time Director of Recreation, a department head position under the City Manager. Why not apply? It was only part time and I could do both jobs, and I felt qualified and it could be challenging. I applied, was interviewed, and was told the city needed to expand the summer and basic kid program, to a full year offering for all ages. I would also help develop parks and develop a community center as funds became available. They asked me if I could meet those requirements. I answered with a confident yes.

Within three months I was asked to accept a full-time position with a substantial salary increase. The city council, the city manager and the residents were pleased with my job performance. I could plan, organize and expand the opportunities for the citizens with a minimal cost to the city. During the following seven years, I developed more community services, including three community parks, two community centers and enhanced the youth, adult and senior citizen programs, more than anyone expected was possible. I was able to accomplish these by forming an alliance with other community organizations. These included; our junior college, the chamber of commerce, the construction team of the Navy Seabees, Kaiser Steel Retirement Association, youth organization leaders and other community leaders and volunteers. This was my most satisfying and rewarding job of all my careers. I was able to use many of my talents and abilities and was a leader in the community. I also was invited and became a member of the service club, Lions International. I served in many office positions, including President.

I left only to get my family out of the California smog and moved to Flagstaff, Arizona in 1978, and without a job. Remember, that at age six, and for approximately seven years, I helped my father do extensive remodeling of our ninety-year-old home? Well, you know as I was helping him, I learned many aspects of the remodeling business. I was soon remodeling residential and commercial properties.

I transferred to the Flagstaff Noon Lions Club but found it difficult to make the mid-day meetings, so I started the Flagstaff Sunrise Lion Club. I became the first president in 1979, and today the club is boasting 78 members, and donates over $150,000 annually.

I bought a dump truck, and this was the beginning of a thirty-year trucking and construction business known as Fast Fred's Incorporated. The one truck increased over time to nineteen. I also expanded operations and became an excavation and grading contractor, a demolition contractor, operated a cinder mine, and a dirt works that produced a balanced and screened top soil mix. Not only did the business require trucks, but graders, back hoes, loaders and screening plants. We had our own office, shop and maintained our equipment on four acres of property. Talk about taking on a large and continuous challenge would be an understatement. My sixty and my wife's fifty-hour weeks were a common occurrence.

I am pleased to state that through personal motivation, all of my varied professions and their successes were made possible by my desire to learn all that I could and to do the best job possible. I had to step out of my comfort zone while taking on new challenges. I always attempted to build my "tools of knowledge," knowing they could be applied in many and various applications. These included taking care of people, while giving attention to details and while planning and streamlining processes.

Today my wife of fifty-five years and I enjoy the ability to do what we want, when we want and not worry about money. I have accomplished my child hood dreams, achieved many expanded goals, and consider my life to be very successful and rewarding.

I am sure you want the best possible life for you and other family members. My book is presented in a comprehensive but direct and simple way. By following and practicing my outlined ideas and procedures, you will accomplish your life's wants and desires.

Yours in success,

Fred

Part 1
About You & Your Powerful Mind

Chapter 1
About You/Us

These are some attributes that I feel are important to me. I assume they may apply to you also.

First, you enjoy a feeling of fulfillment when you have accomplished a great undertaking, you feel happy and joyful. It may be that you have gained some financial freedom or attained other rewards, such as; acknowledgment, praise, accolades or approval.

Second, you like to be appreciated for your accomplishments and know you are appreciated even for a small contribution or effort.

Third, you enjoy giving love as well as receiving love and intimacy. Love is the root and the foundation of all life throughout the universe and has been taught by the mystics throughout history.

Fourth, you enjoy health, and if a health challenge is within your current situation, you look forward to being well again.

Fifth, you love your family and friends (at least your grandchildren and most others) and enjoy expanding and growing your relationships with friends and family. I will expand on the importance of having good family and friendships under the chapter of forgiveness.

Sixth, you probably enjoy feeling spiritual and close to your creator and your surroundings, you have an appreciation for the great universe that we share with other beings and all other living life forms, including plants and animals.

Seventh, you love feeling mentally adept and alert. Things just seem to go smoother and work out better with this frame of mind.

Eighth, you do not like the feeling of being in a rut (a grave with the ends removed). You dislike the feeling of going nowhere or working too hard at trying to get where you want to go.

Ninth, you want to improve yourself and you know how important your motivation and knowledge is to your success.

As I was developing "About Us," I considered what were the most important or rewarding feelings that have contributed to my personality, feelings and my personal success. I looked at what assisted me in striving forward in my endeavors, to have the energy, enthusiasm and confidence to step forward beyond my comfort zone and try new things in life. As you may have discovered in my autobiography, I proceeded to take on challenges that helped me grow and advanced me to even greater "avenues" of personal successes. I then realized that these were not only my basic attributes, but I have observed that almost everyone has the same attributes or feeling to some degree. Take a few moments to analyze to what degree they have contributed to your thinking and to your life.

Part one will explain how and where these become a part of "You" and how you develop them, and how the "mind programing" is so important to your "success".

Part two will present eight avenues to your greater success that I feel everyone should possess in order to attain the life they desire. They are presented in what I call the "Eight Success Essentials" and are much greater in detail than found in this introductory chapter.

Part three helps you to determine where you are today, where you want to go and what you wish to accomplish in life. It will lead you step by step in establishing your goals that you may wish to pursue in life.

Part four supplies the forms that will help you prioritize, organize and lead you to your desires. Following the forms (copy, enlarge and create your own work book), are affirmations and daily guides that are extremely helpful in generating successful thoughts that produce success.

Chapter 2
Success, Abundance and Mind

Each of us picture success in an individual and unique way that is meaningful to us. It may mean financial independence, or it may mean achievement of your desires and goals in the areas of your life. It may mean developing friendships or harmony within your family; it's your choice and yours alone. To me success is the progressive movement toward my personal goals and seeing them manifest in one or more of my 8 areas of my life. This means that I believe I am successful as I complete each step toward my goal, not only when I attain the major goal. I will introduce the 8 areas later. Your ideas of having a successful life will begin to move you toward those wants and desires.

Your ideas of success must first become established in your conscious mind. This is your rational and creative mind that you have control over. You program it in the way you see or interpret what you see. It highly depends on whether you are a positive or negative person; more on this later.

What you are thinking and envisioning in your conscious mind is transmitted automatically into your subconscious, or in metaphysical terms, your subjective mind. Positive thinking will greatly assist bringing you your desired success. Your subjective mind is your "God" mind. It relates to the higher power. Your subjective mind always has the answer, and the answer to your thought is always yes. What you believe is what you get and become. The subjective mind is more powerful than your subconscious mind when you believe God has the answers. Both minds accept your ideas and thoughts and are working continuously in the manifestation of your thoughts.

The statement "I am" is a very powerful expression. If you say, "I am tired, ill, or sick of this or that", the answer will be yes. If you say, "I am healthy, wealthy, wise, full or energy and joyful," the answer will be yes. Your statements manifest in your life in the manor expressed.

Are your thoughts taking you toward the goals or outcomes that you want? Are your thoughts positive or negative, on success or on failure, on love or hate, or on the ugliness or the beauty surrounding you? All change comes from within you, starting with your conscious mind and what you place in it. I could not have changed professions and advanced my professional life without possessing the above positive attributes.

Now let us consider abundance. What does it mean to be abundant? Is it abundance that you are after, or is it simply money? To most, abundance means money, but if you really think about it, it is much more than that. It includes fine relationships, family cohesion, social acceptance, good mental ability, health, happiness, creative freedom, and a great spiritual life. Abundance can be found everywhere the eye can see and beyond and is available to each of us. But many of us block this natural state with negative thoughts such as: I am not worthy or deserving, others have it all, I am just unlucky when it comes to receiving good. Many believe abundance cannot create happiness and they may be right, but it sure is a good start in having a life that lacks in very few wants and needs. It may eliminate a lot of frustration and anxieties that do not attract the best to your life.

Your conscious mind must mentally accept the flow of abundance into your life. You also must feel that you are worthy and deserve an abundant life. There must also be the necessary activity or action on your part, both mentally and physically to bring that flow about. For example; just thinking abundance will not fill your bank account, but your proper way of thinking will direct you into channels of activity whereby your bank account may be enhanced. You must first know that you need some extra cash, state the reason, and then state the desired amount. The action may take some time; a few more house calls, producing more items for sale, or simply having a garage sale.

Many say that the love of money is the root of all evil, but they overlook the fact that in all probability it is not the money, but the way individuals may sometimes use it that might be termed evil. Other negative beliefs that might inhibit you from financial abundance are: I don't deserve it, we may not be rich, but we are honest (therefore, if you are rich you must be dishonest), money does not grow on trees, you must work hard for money. Don't let these beliefs and other limiting thoughts create lack in your life.

Actually, money is nothing more than tangible evidence of the service you have rendered to another or society. In the world where the medium of exchange is money, it is natural for you to receive money in return for a specific commodity or service you offer. There is always enough money to go around.

Let me point out two more mistaken beliefs about money. I have talked to people who feel that the rich people have most of the money and therefore it deprives the less fortunate of possessing adequate financial success. They are blaming external circumstances. They are not taking personal responsibility for their lack of successful thoughts and planning for a better financial wellbeing. Those "hording" money or not investing their assets, are doing so only if they are storing their money under the mattress or in their safe. The real picture is, (eliminating money hoarders) those possessing the money are spending it on more than just paying the rent, putting food on the table, paying a car payment, and taking an occasional ride or venture. They spend money on more luxurious items or vacations, boats, aircraft, recreational vehicles, yard upgrades, dining out often, going to resorts or cruises to other lands. All of these are sharing their wealth with others by distributing their wellbeing and putting people to work and creating jobs. It is said that each dollar spent circulates at least seven times, thus helping many during this sequence.

The second mistaken belief is in scarcity, which is the belief in personal lack projected onto one's environment. Money is just an idea or tool to use to spend on that which you desire or need. Most financial transactions are performed electronically from one account to another including credit card use. Most people have but a few dollars in their purse or wallet but have at least one credit card. The use of the credit card buys you up to thirty days of other peoples' money, and if paid in full each month, it is like using cash without a transaction fee or interest.

The entire universe and everything within it show us abundance everywhere we look. Can you count the stars in the sky, the grains of sand on a beach, the trees in a forest, ears of corn in a field, the acres of water in the oceans, the wild life within the forest, or the many people we encounter each week? Our farmers produce enough food to feed our country and other nations' needs. Abundance is seen everywhere with the right thinking and perspective. Why should you not experience abundance?

Now let us look at the term success. This is a good time to look at your definition of success. Spend a few relaxed and quiet minutes just dreaming about what you consider successful, and how you would define success.

Write your current definition of success here:

My definition of success is, "Doing what you want, when you want, without worrying about the how". You cannot worry how you will be able to accomplish your desires and wants without enough time, money or if you might fail. These are instructions to your subconscious mind to produce failures. These are all roadblocks to your ultimate success and fall under negative thinking, which produce negative results.

Many look for success in remote areas. Some move from place to place, thinking "the grass is greener elsewhere," or there are better opportunities beyond the horizon. Minister and educator Russell H. Conwell delivered his famous motivational lecture, "Acres of Diamonds" in the late 1870's. He insisted that success can be found right where you stand, providing you possess the simplicity and soundness of character to see it. He taught that wealth comes from filling a genuine human need and using your products and earnings to support the betterment of others. These earnings are produced through proper thinking, the discovery of your wants and desires and the use of your talents and abilities.

You have been developing the "know how" to accomplish what you want out of life beginning at an early age. You have developed the ability to successfully meet challenges as they presented themselves to you. The way you think and the way you handle your life challenges are what brings you success or failure.

I remember when I went on my first date in the 7th grade. I did not know what to expect or what to say, so I did not say much, and I felt awkward during my time with her. After my parents and I returned her home, I began to think how I could do better next time. I planned the next date in my head and asked my parents what I could do better. The next date went much better because I had a little more confidence through planning. I had better thoughts of success and less of failure.

Work on bettering your life, and by following the ideas in this book, I promise it will pay large dividends now and later. Remember to live the best life possible, for this life is not a dress rehearsal.

Summary Questions
Chapter 2-Success, Abundance and Mind

What is my picture of a successful life?

What does an abundant life look like to me?

What do I want out of life?

What talents and abilities am I using in life?

What am I selling as a product or service?

Is my definition of success compatible with my above answers, or do I need to change some parts of it?

Chapter 3
Your Beautiful and Creative Mind

Your mind is the most beautiful, transformative tool you have. Even the most powerful computers cannot stand up to the magnificence of your mind. Your mind's capacity and abilities are still not fully comprehended by the greatest minds of all time. Einstein proclaimed he only used approximately five percent of his mind's capacity.

We should envision our mind as focused on and attuned to our highest and best good. It is working for us, in wanting a good life. A well-trained mind will bring you greater results than you can imagine. Training your mind to be conscious of what you desire at any given moment enables you to see, recognize and comprehend what is necessary to bring to you, your highest and best results. You must understand your desires and how these desires manifest in your life.   You must become aware of your thoughts and become aware of that which you are looking for, so when the answers present themselves, you will recognize them.

For example, when I was Director of Recreation and Parks for the city of Upland California, I would meet with groups and leaders of youth, adults and senior organizations. This helped me to stay informed of their present and future needs.   At a meeting with the American Youth Soccer Association, they informed me that they would need additional playing fields within two years. (I started AYSO in Upland and they grew to 7000 players in the seven years that I was with the city). My mind was now aware of a need. I had a three-acre neighborhood park site that could be developed when funds became available. The problem was I had limited funds and there was a major rock pile on the site. It came to my mind from my naval days, that the Navy had a construction division known as the Sea Bees. They agreed to conduct training exercises consisting of two weekends and removed the rock pile and did the rough grading at no cost to the city.

During the next meeting with AYSO, I told them I would budget for a small parking lot, a playground area and rest room facilities. I asked them if they could develop the three grass playing fields, with fencing, irrigation, and an asphalt parking lot. They answered yes if I could come up with the money for the light fixtures, poles, wiring and light panels for one field. I met them half way financially, knowing that they could get their half covered through donations. We all had a goal in mind, answers and steps toward the achievement of the goal presented themselves and all were prepared to recognize them. Within two years the teams were playing on the fields. As a bonus, the neighborhood had a park and they were no longer looking at a rock pile and dirt field. Many opportunities pass us by because we are not prepared for them.

Your life is a reflection of your consciousness. You are what you have become and where you are today through the sum total of your previous thoughts. Your thoughts have manifested into actions. The way you interpret what you see, is what you become. You also meet life's challenges through how you have programmed or prepared your mind to envision and interpret what is happening to you.

Some people find excuses and fault outside of themselves. It is easy to blame others or circumstances for their ill-fate, failures or bad choices. A well rounded and more knowledgeable person takes responsibility for what is happening to him or her.

In dealing with personal situations or an argument with another or others, you must first determine what percentage of this is your fault or doing? You may have erroneously accepted the word of another or misinterpreted or perceived the circumstance incorrectly. You may have been hurt or the situation may have violated your way of thinking or understanding, or the outcome was undesirable. You will find that you are 1-99% at fault. With this understanding, you are in a position to understand the outcome or apologize for your part of the argument. In dealing with an argument, this generally leads to an understanding or solves the conflict. If the other participant does not reciprocate, then it is time to escape from the situation. One of my favorite sayings is "You never get in a pissing contest with a skunk, because there are no winners." In dealing with a personal negative situation, you become more aware of the reason for the outcome. You are now in a better position to make corrections.

To make corrections, it is necessary to change the way you think. What you think is the cause and the outcome is the effect. To change your way of thinking, or real belief system is probably the most difficult thing you can ever attempt. It is easier to blame mom, dad, the government, or the "devil" for all your woes. Ernest Holmes, founder of Religious Science, (now known as Centers for Spiritual Living) stated, "To learn how to think is to learn how to live." He also said, "To change your mind (the way you think) is to change your life."

Earnest Holmes was a well-known author and wrote the Science of Mind text book. He was a gifted scholar with an extensive knowledge of the world's spiritual philosophies and an expert in spiritual psychology. He had his own radio program, gave lectures and seminars and wrote many books. He was one of several metaphysicians that were instrumental in the development of the New Thought movement. He taught how your mind is also related to God's mind.

I have been a student of Religious Science and it has taught me how to increase and use my mental power to positively change my life. It can change your life by following and practicing these and other principles I present in this book. Each chapter is dedicated to help you to ensure that you become the best you, and you accomplish your wants and desires.

Just make up your mind right now that you are taking full control of your life and your future. Changing your thinking is a must if you are to advance your life in a more positive and dynamic way. This means you will no longer blame others or outside circumstances for your short comings. You must step into the greater truth of who you are and how you think. You are not bound by the so-called past because you are no longer the same person that you were even yesterday, because every day brings changes in your life. So, move forward toward a greater and more abundant life through expanded and positive thinking, and have fun while doing so.

Our thoughts are the food of our beliefs. What we believe is the food of our creation and what actually shows up in physical form. We can change what we experience in our lives because we can change our thoughts. When we practice changing our beliefs, it will ultimately change our life experience.

All change comes from within you and starts by thoughts you hold in mind. These thoughts have brought you to what you have been, what you are, and what you will become. The mind will work for or against you in direct accordance to what you believe. You have known people that believe that nothing is right in the world or in their life. Sure enough, little goes right for them. Others you know look at the best of life and their surroundings and give thanks for that which occurs in their life; and life is good. If you believe in yourself, your abilities and the greatness around you, you possess a positive and successful outlook, you will attract all that you desire throughout your life. I certainly hope you associate with positive and successful people. The negative people are annoying and can undermine your positive mental attitude.

If you let yourself believe you are surrounded by lack and limitations, all you will attract is a world that only brings you hurt and limitations. Successful people think positive thoughts of success. This is the foundation or principle that all top athletes, racers of all kinds, top executives and successful people have in common. A successful person is filled with a subtle something which permeates everything that he does with an atmosphere of confidence and strength. He knows that with the right thinking, planning, organization, and the use of his talents and abilities, he is destined to succeed.

Once you decide to use your mind constructively, you become stronger and more capable than ever before. To hold ideas of success will bring good to you. To know this will bring you joy and happiness. What you see is what you get. What you think is what you become. So it is of the utmost importance that you predominately see and think the good within you, others and your surroundings.

All actions are first created in mind and may be called first cause. First cause is the input of thought in your conscious mind—the way and what you think. This mind is where the idea, then the thought is developed and analyzed. This is your conscious mind that you rationally understand and control. It is also known as the creative mind. It is then automatically accepted by your subconscious mind, your subliminal (God Mind) also known as your subjective mind. These minds never rest, are always active. These minds manifest your thoughts into actions that directly relate to the way you chose to entertain that idea.   Was it a positive and a successful idea or a negative idea? This will determine the type of outcome you will receive that will be manifested in your life.   This is known as the effect of your idea or thought. This process is known as cause and effect.   Dr. Terry Cole Whittaker states, "You can foretell your future simply by examining your thoughts.   Where have your mind, emotions, and imaginations been taking you? Unless we know who we are, we are subject to mind programming through whatever we watch, hear, see, believe, and then we follow up with action."

Once you know how to use your mind to your advantage and well-being, why would you ever go back to your old negative thoughts that have been detrimental to your greater success? One of the greatest gifts you have is the power of choice.   You can choose to think positive and creative thoughts that enhance your life in a successful way.   You can also choose to limit your well-being through negative, hurtful and unproductive thoughts.

Summary Questions
Chapter 3-Your Beautiful and Creative Mind

Which way of thinking do you prefer?

To be more positive in my outlook on life, I need to:

To manifest a more successful and abundant life, I need to:

How would I feel to have my mind working for me producing positive effects (manifestations) in my life?

Chapter 4
Ideas

Your ideas and how you perceived and accepted them played an important part in your personal growth and habit formations. Some ideas started to develop during your early childhood, as you advanced in life and continued to develop daily. These ideas or thoughts have led you to become all that you are today.

Be sure to accept the ideas and thoughts herein that will lead you to your better self. You must avoid any ideas of doubt, lack, being unworthy or of hatred. Ideas should support your self-esteem and your trust in yourself and your abilities.

A powerful way to bring about new ideas is by escaping to a quiet space, clear your mind, relax and concentrate on breathing, exhaling tension and worries. You may walk a labyrinth, voice a mantra, drum, sing or walk. While relaxing, just let your mind wander. Ideas may become crystal clear or may present themselves in a subtle way. Intuition may present feelings, ideas, or solutions. If these are heartfelt and move you, you should act on them with a plan of action that will be presented in Part III.

Where are ideas lost and never realized, even if we really desire them? You may want reinforcement from another or others. This is only a good move if the person or persons support you and the idea. Be careful when sharing your idea with others. You cannot be certain that in most cases, they will positively support and help you realize your idea or dream. If the person gives you negative feedback, giving you all kinds of reasons, it is a bad idea and why it will not work, you are likely to abandon it.

Now what you do with the idea is critical. First of all, I would only seek professional assistance, and not seek support mentioned above. If you treat it like a new years' resolution, stating I will do this or that or you sit on it without writing it down, it may be lost from thought in a short time. Without creating a written goal and giving it urgency by establishing a deadline, it will not likely come about.

The very worst thing you can do is to doubt yourself and your ability to achieve your idea, goal or desire. I strongly believe that you cannot conceive an idea that you do not have the ability to solve or create. The doubts come from fearing failure. By stating such blockers as: I don't deserve or am unworthy, I do not have enough time, I am swamped already, I do not have enough money to follow through with the idea, it is too great a task for me, others may think it is a dumb idea, or it will not work, or if it were a great idea others would have already done it, are real stoppers.

We all want our dreams to come true, but many people hesitate before taking action. They procrastinate, uncertain of what to do. Most procrastination is based on avoiding an irrational fear that something may go wrong and is usually driven by self-doubt or poor self-esteem.

There is also a powerful connection between perfectionism and procrastination. For the perfectionist, there is never enough information acquired to move forward on the idea, and that form of thinking undermines your confidence and self-esteem and can lead to procrastination. Do you need more information? Gather it. But remember: you can never have "enough" information to guarantee 100 percent success.

Life is a matter of action and you must be an active participant, not a bystander waiting for things to be done for you. If you just sit and wait, you will progress very little. You must find new ideas, better ways of doing things in almost every phase of your endeavors, whether in business affairs, rendering a service to others, or in family affairs, etc. You will find all that you can do, all the progress that you can make, depends upon the ideas you may be able to summon up out of your mind and rightly apply to the endeavor confronting you.

A personal example of taking action and coming up with an idea and applying it toward a personal desire is my box boy story. I was a junior in high school and a new grocery store advertised for employees including box boys (now called baggers). I needed that job and to demonstrate this, I came to the interview dressed in a coat and tie. Two others also dressed in like manner and all three of us were hired along with six others out of approximately thirty-five applicants. We had found a way to stand out from the others and to make a good impression.

It is of the utmost importance that what you think must be positive only. Be careful of what you think and say because that is what you become and that which will manifest in your life. Eric Butterworth stated, "By your thinking, you are either adding to your good or you are taking away from it. Failure or lack in your life is the result of continuously 'minus-ing' yourself." Remember, Dr. Ernest Holmes stated, "Change your thinking is to change your life." He also proclaimed, "All thought is creative." Be positive in what you think and the way you think because that is what will create your way of life.

The cause and effect rule is very important to remember. Cause is your thoughts placed into your conscious mind and it is accepted, and it programs your subconscious mind. The effect is the manifestation, outcome or result of your expressions or thoughts. Positive thoughts result in positive actions. Negative thoughts result in failures, hurtful events, upsets, disease and trauma (including loss of friends). I cannot over emphasize the importance of positive and successful attitudes and consciousness to bring you the life you want and deserve.

Your life today is the sum total of all your previous thoughts, which became manifest in your life. You are and have been living the effects of all your thoughts.

The good news is most of you had predominately good thoughts and had positive life results. Your negative thoughts have brought about experiences that did not work well for you and you would like to have changed them or would like to change them now so there will not be future negative experiences in your life. Now is the time to change your thoughts to positive thinking. But remember, we must live our life today and the past is behind us (unless you continue to relive or dwell on the negative past, which will require work and healing on your part).

How you have handled the past negative experiences made a great difference in your life's development. Did you or do you look at these so-called failures as a learning experience, challenge, or as failure? It is never too late to readjust your way of approaching life and go positive. George Bernard Shaw stated, "Life isn't about finding yourself. Life is about creating yourself."

Remember, the world is changing around us, and we are influenced by and challenged by these changes. If you are to keep up with society, technology, and keep up with your wants, desires and goals, you must continue to change and recreate your thinking and your life. You must grow in the direction of your choosing. Socrates said, "The secret to change is to focus all your energy, not of fighting the old, but building on the new."

Summary Questions
Chapter 4-Ideas

How can I bring about new ideas?

How can I protect my ideas?

How can I avoid procrastinating?

Do I need to change my thinking, if so, to what?

What in life do I need to keep up with the changes around me?

Would keeping a note pad and writing down ideas help me to retain and move forward on them?

How can I become more positive in my way of looking at life?

Chapter 5
Success and Mediocrity

There are two types of successes gained by people. One is being better than others in a competitive way. The other is a person who brings forth from within himself in an expressive or gainful manner that is personally satisfying to him. It could be in helping his fellow man or his community. He may demonstrate leadership and possess confidence in all of his activities. He does not measure his success by comparing his performance to others.

This is a competitive world and most want to outperform others. It may require having a slight edge over what others may be doing. It is putting a little more time, effort, organizing, planning, thought and practice (especially goal setting) than others are willing to do that places you ahead of the also-rans. More importantly, it brings personal satisfaction and self-esteem.

The slight edge can be seen in sports, business or even marriage. The winning horse, car, or athlete may come in first place by a nose, tenth of a second or by some other measurement, receiving twice the fame and fortune. They are not twice as good as the second placer but possess that slight edge. The most successful business owners, the person that gets the promotion or receives the hand in marriage, all possess the slight edge.

Demonstrating a great personality will attract people to you and their desire to associate or to do business with you. This is also a great asset to develop, giving you a slight edge. My definition of personality is, "Your outer expression of your inner attitude." A positive attitude and success consciousness are the foundation of your personality.

Good salesmanship, the ability to persuade others to accept your attributes, ideas or purchase your product or service, is also known to give you that slight edge.

Success builds upon success because the person who knows success has developed successful habits and ways of thinking that work for him. That person does not interrupt the flow of success with ideas of failure. On the other hand, a person who is experiencing failure can stop the downward trend by realizing that thoughts of failure produce habits that produce unsuccessful events. They can reverse this by concentrating on the development of positive attitudes and success consciousness building.

The difference between being successful or being just mediocre is always a choice. If you just go with the flow, doing what is only required of you, never stepping out of your comfort zone and trying new challenges or experiences in your life, then you will be with the other also-rans. You will, unknowingly, not receive the more abundant and successful life that you dream of having and that you deserve. Many opportunities will pass you by without you even being aware of them.

In Part II, I will present to you what I have found that all successful people have in common. I call them the Eight Success Essentials.   Together they will lead you to great success and desired accomplishments.

They are:

1. **Positive Mental Attitude:** The way you see and express all events in your life.
2. **Success Consciousness:** You only have successful thoughts in all you think and do.
3. **Understanding:** There is a Power throughout the Universe that guides us, loves us-many people call it God.
4. **Thankfulness:** Demonstrating an attitude of gratitude.
5. **Forgiveness:** Forgiving yourself and others.
6. **Service to others.**
7. **Selective Giving:** Of your resources.
8. **Goal Setting:** Starting by placing in writing, your wants and desires and follow up with action.

You may agree with all or most of these and you may feel that there are others that you would add such as: education, reading books and joining a master mind group. The eight noted are the ones I have found to be of greatest value to my own and others success.

Summary Questions
Chapter 5-Success and Mediocrity

What must I do to become more successful?

1.

2.

3.

4.

5.

Part 2
The Eight Success Essentials

Chapter 6
Positive Mental Attitude

In part 1, I laid the ground work for Part 2, especially for this and the following chapter. I attempted not to be redundant in my presentation. Remember, an attitude means a position assumed, or studied, as indicating action feeling or mood. Your mental attitude, then, is the general tendency of your mind to respond to or act upon your thoughts. These thoughts are a positive or negative way of interpreting or visioning what is happening in your life and your surroundings. You have the freedom to choose how you respond and react to your circumstances and situations. How you choose to see life in general, will become the way you think and these thoughts manifest in your life. Your attitude is the key ingredient that makes up your personality, and is evident to others, whether you have a dynamic and positive personality or a negative one. It is natural that people wish to associate with the person that possesses a positive mental attitude. How you look at life and your surroundings, is what develops within you; a positive or negative mental attitude.

If you can see love, beauty, the good in people, all events as good or challenging, it will lead you to developing a positive mental attitude. It will generally lead you to a successful and prosperous life.

If you see hate, ugliness in your surroundings, the worst in people, and visualize a problem in everything you see, you will develop a negative mental attitude. This will naturally bring you only hurt and discontent.

How you look at life will become the way you think and how you envision life to be. This will be the path your life will follow and what you will become. You can see a glass of water as being half full (which is positive), or as being half empty (negative), demonstrates your perspective and of your way of looking at things. They are both correct, but which way do you want to look at life and become?

How you see yourself becomes your experience. When you release your negative thoughts and emotions, such as fear and your belief in lack and limitation, your life begins to reflect the good that you desire. You do this by practicing and entertaining positive thoughts through repetition, it becomes your new habit of thinking. People will want to associate with you and help you. No one wants to be around one that practices self-pity and is a "go nowhere" in life person.

All thought is creative, according to the inputs, emotions or conviction behind the thought. Just because your father and mother died at an early age, or they were overweight, you should not expect to suffer the same fate. What your mind expects for your body and your life to become, is what you will manifest due to your way of thinking. If you believe in longevity of life, and you eat healthy foods, then you will certainly receive a much different outcome.

Developing a positive mental attitude is definitely an asset that will bring to you great rewards in life. It also gives you an advantage to become the person you wish to become.

Summary Questions
Chapter 6-Positive Mental Attitude

1. Are my thoughts and beliefs leading me to success? If not, what must I do to change them?

2. Is my mental attitude positive? If not, what must I change?

3. Is my personality attracting? If not, what must I do?

4. I can improve my thought and mental attitude therefore my life by:

    1.

    2.

    3.

    4.

Chapter 7
Success Consciousness

Return to Part 1, Chapter 2, and review your definition of success. It should move you and give you urgency to continue forward. Your success consciousness plays an important part in your acquisition of your dream of success.

Success is personal and found within your being. Success is a matter of attitude and consciousness. It is also a journey of planning and actions toward personal development. This is where programming your subconscious mind through positive thoughts will produce within you a consciousness of success. By repeating to yourself, "I can be a success; I will succeed in all that I choose to accomplish," is a great way to build your success consciousness.

The habitual thinking of having a successful life will create success. Habitual is the key word. It is said that 95% of what we do is by habit. While learning to drive a car, to type, ride a bicycle, developing communication skills, etc., we must practice it over and over again until it becomes accurate, safe, successful and automatic. It also becomes much faster, less stressful and more efficient, giving us the ability to perform additional tasks.

To develop success consciousness, you must create the habit of successful thinking, build self-confidence and know you are a winner. When playing in an open tennis tournament (open to world players), I found myself playing center court (bleachers surrounding the court) and against the number 16th ceded player. The stands were full of spectators and if I had lost my confidence and success consciousness (the common word is choked), I would have lost miserably and would have disappointed many people. Instead, I played the best game ever and lost by close games in all three sets.

Even though I lost that match, I felt like a winner because I knew I had performed well.

Dr. Terry Cole Whittaker tells a story asking you to think back when you were a sperm. She stated that there is enough sperm in a thimble to populate the world. You as a sperm ran the greatest race of your life and against the greatest odds ever and you beat all the others to the egg. You see, you are a winner and you did not realize it. There are no losers in this world, only winners but many don't realize this fact and therefore many don't win often.

You must build success consciousness by understanding all that you have learned and accomplished in life. You have been learning from many sources, including learning from past mistakes and what you perceived as failures. These were learning experiences and you overcame them by rethinking and redoing them. What you have learned I call your "tools of knowledge" that you now can use in problem solving and will help you to achieve your needs and desires. If you use what you have learned, and your knowledge gained the outcome will be successful in all that you attempt in life. In my life, for example, every job or position I applied for, I received. Every venture I entered was highly successful and was personally gratifying because I am success oriented. You too must advance and build your success consciousness. That will bring you even greater successes in your life.

To advance your life, you must step out of your comfort zone and tackle new and challenging things. I suppose I began this process, as found in my autobiography, with my first grade Myrna Hughes story, when I decided to become the best I could be. Larry the cable guy, the well-known comedian says, "Just git-err done." You cannot get it done by procrastinating, only by getting started today.

Summary Questions
Chapter 7-Success Consciousness

1.Am I a self-starter or do I need to become one?

2. Is my attitude supporting my development of a greater success consciousness?

3. What negative habits of thought do I need to overcome to be more success conscious?

4. What positive habits are producing and supporting my success consciousness?

5. I feel that I am a winner because:

6. If not, why not?

Chapter 8
A Power that Guides Us

The greatest mystics including Jesus, Buddha, Hafiz, Einstein, Ernest Holmes, Rumi, Moses, Plato, Socrates, Aristotle, Goethe, Emerson, Whitman, Browning and many others have all taught and proclaimed, there is a Great Power, Universal Mind, Creator, Supreme Intelligence, and Universal Energy that is powerful, loving, and is a positive and creative force in our life. Many call this great power God.

This God power is so great it influences your life to the degree of your recognition of It. As you achieve greater understanding of the teachings of the mystics and the laws and principles, greater manifestations will result. These principles include: God is all there is, God is Love, God expresses through you and me, God always wants the best for us, and always says yes to our thoughts and expressions. The more you embody these, the greater they will become a guiding factor in your life.

This is another reason to be positive and have success consciousness. If you say you are not happy, have little money, may become or are ill, or people don't treat you fairly, you are not happy in the job or position you hold, or you are always tired, the answer will be yes you are right.

The way you think is the way your life will turn out. Here is where cause and effect play a major role in your life. The thought (cause) is the instruction to God and your subliminal mind to create or act upon that thought. This sets in motion the manifestation of that thought, known as effect.

Focus all your powers on where you are going and what you desire in your heart. Then act that way instead of worrying. A problem in any form is not complicated but is easy to solve when you know it for what it is-a concept, a belief, a game of right and wrong, or something first mentally created by you or someone else.

We are God species, and with our mystic powers, we can co-create with our Source whenever we desire and put into motion our thoughts, words, intentions or actions. Eileen Caddy, in her book, "The Dawn of Changes" writes, "You are never asked to do more than you are able without being given the strength and ability to do it." I would also suggest that you follow any intuition you may receive, because as Wayne Dyer pointed out, "It came to you through God's Mind."

To realize the great God power surrounding each of us, look at the magnificence within the universe and the balance of our solar system. Meditate in a quiet place in your yard or garden, forest, a library, on a lake, under the stars, walking a labyrinth, drumming, or doing a mantra. Just let your mind see the dynamics and beauty surrounding you and the astonishing results of nature and that which is all life and all Love and God. Great positive thoughts and solutions may present themselves unexpectedly. Remember to appreciate their source and give thanks.

Summary Questions
Chapter 8-A Power that Guides Us

1.Do I believe this to be one of my success essentials? If not, why not?

2.Is there anything I need to change in my belief in the Power?

3.What if anything, must I do to help this Power work for me?

Chapter 9
Forgiveness

Forgiveness is probably the most difficult habit, feeling and expression to nurture and expand of the eight success essentials. The main reason is that your thinking or habit of thought has been in judging others. Another reason is your ego has been hurt and you need to blame the person that violated your way of thinking or the way you performed. This has brought about the actualization of negative thoughts and undermined your attitude toward that person. You get revenge through retaliatory actions, (remember that thoughts manifest into actions) in order to reciprocate. This can also be thought avoidance or not speaking to them. These decisions always lead you down the path of more ill feelings or resentments.

If you want to experience deep abiding tranquility, you will not find it by clinging to anger, fear or through judgment. It begins within your way of thinking. You must accept that we are all individuals and express ourselves in different ways. We cannot show bias toward others. Ralph Waldo Emerson stated, "For every minute you are angry, you lose sixty-seconds of happiness."

You may seek justification from others to prove you are correct in your feelings or actions toward the hurtful person. People who have your best interest in mind may say your emotions are justified. They may urge you to continue believing that the person doesn't deserve forgiveness. I believe everyone deserves forgiveness. I also believe you deserve forgiveness. You deserve the freedom from the pain you have been carrying. Your holding onto grudges, stops the flow of your good.

Forgiveness is the process of releasing the demands and expectations we place on others that create separation between two people. These negative expectations block the path of love, which should be your natural state of being. Love is the essence of who you are and what you are made of. One cannot truly forgive without being compassionate and loving.

Grudges, hate, discontents are just mental clutter of old ideas. Although we may not be aware that we are holding onto these old ways of thinking, they continue to affect our choices and behavior. An example of this mental clutter is the belief that forgiveness means condoning a destructive act. It is far more productive to think of this as past history or that it may have had a constructive outcome, or helped someone grow, otherwise it takes away positive energy. It definitely affects your mental attitude and your personality. Remember the definition of personality. Forgiveness is our choice to release judgment and to embrace the past, finding the gift or lesson in what occurred and moving lovingly forward, knowing that anything is possible for us. Mark Twain said, "Forgiveness is the fragrance that the violet sheds on the heel that has crushed it."

We must remember we each are God's children; we are all brothers. We need to be kind to one another; isn't this what we want from others? We each experience life in a unique way. Our experiences have affected the way we have grown personally and the way we express and handle life situations. This is why we approach challenges and expressions differently than others may.

We are all human and we all make mistakes. The starting point for creating a better future for ourselves is to deliberately free our mind from the mistakes of yesterday. They need no longer be held against you; they need no longer be a liability. You are not a failure if the previous choices you made brought you ill results. You must treat them as a learning experience. Holding ill feelings toward yourself and others will definitely contribute to disruptions in family, friendships and the work place. Some carry these ill feelings forever and never get over their mistakes or grudges, which negatively affects them the rest of their life.

Too often, our minds are so burdened because of the mistakes we have made, we do not take time to forgive ourselves and others and start over again. And so, it is wise to occasionally review the past and try to find out just what we have been thinking and doing to create this burden in our mind.

Forgiveness and forgetting is a gift you should give to yourself in order to be free. Confucius stated it well, "He who cannot forgive others breaks the bridge over which he himself must pass." Forgiving those who you believe have done something undesirable to you, frees up your attention so you can focus on making your life better. Abstention from your judging of others requires disciplined thinking that will produce clear and constant standards of personal behavior. This habit of thinking will lead you to being kind and forgiving.

Remember, the beginning step to forgiveness is you must forgive yourself for past decisions that you would like to have done differently. Life is always a challenge and a learning process. The only way to ensure that you don't make mistakes is to do nothing new in life, and this will create a life of no progress. Take steps toward new adventures that present themselves to you. This will take you to a life of progress, expansion and success.

You are bound to make mistakes, be criticized by others, but you have learned to regroup, analyze what went wrong and make corrections, either consciously or unconsciously and you moved forward in life. The greatest correction that you can make is the development of your positive thinking. This will lead you to create an attitude of loving yourself and those who made the mistake that violated you in some way.

Since the present is our only power, and today is the only day in which we live, and yesterday has forever passed, the change within ourselves must be made today.

If you blame others for what went wrong, then there are no corrections made. If you do not accept some degree of responsibility, you do not need to change your thinking or action. There is a saying: while you were busy judging others, you left your closet open and your skeletons fell out. Another is: if only closed minds came with closed mouths. There are always many sides or points of view to every misunderstanding.

Understanding this, the very first question for you to consider is: what percentage of the problem is mine? It could be 1% to 99%. You now have a greater understanding of the mishap or conflict that occurred in the beginning.

It is now time to take that step forward and apologize to the person or persons, for not understanding the extent of your action or reaction and how it may have contributed to the hurtful situation. They may unload or express their feelings; do not add fuel to the fire by getting upset or retaliate. Now is the time to provide a listening ear and offer your warm and peaceful presence. You may want to jump in and fix or correct the persons misunderstanding. Even the best intentions may cause further upset if your advice or actions are not warranted or asked for. A good way to conflict resolution is to say yes or agree with the person. How then can the person disagree with you? This will open the door to communications with the other person. Naturally, you want to be tactful and avoid upsetting him or flaring up the dispute.

At this time, they may apologize for their role or interference or their part in the conflict. Game over.

You should understand that others have been having life experiences that affect the way they say and act in certain circumstances. They may be critical of the way you perform because they do it differently. Their mistake is trying to impose their way upon you and they probably don't know better. Remember there are no winners in the get even game. Trying to get even will negatively affect your attitude, your health, your family and your other relationships. If you hold onto grudges, then the situation cannot be cured. "You will know that forgiveness has begun when you recall those who hurt you and feel the power to wish them well," Lewis B. Smedes.

Summary Questions
Chapter 9-Forgiveness

1.How can I become a more forgiving person?

2.What do I need to do to be less judgmental?

3.What do I regret saying or doing that I need to forgive myself?

4.What angers or fears must I address in my life?

5.What demands or expectations toward others must I change?

6. What must I do to enhance good family relations?

7.Who do I need to forgive? How do I plan to do so?

Chapter 10
Thanksgiving

Giving thanks for the small as well as the greater happenings in your life are the very basics for attracting even more and greater ones to your life. It shows your appreciation for the blessings received. The appropriate response to God's will to give is an essential aspect to love, which brings joy to those who give it as well as those who receive it.

When you give thanks for the parking space, the stars, the flowers, for your friends, the weather, the beautiful sunset, the lakes and forest, your car and home, that you woke up this morning, will create the habit of giving thanks. Giving thanks for the beauty and abundance surrounding you will also lead to a more rewarding and abundant life. Remember thoughts are attracting.

An attitude of gratitude demonstrates your appreciation for all that is, has been and is manifesting in your life. It shows your willingness to accept God's gifts. Remember that you must ask to receive.

Wayne Dyer said, "The nature of gratitude helps dispel the idea that we do not have enough, that we will never have enough, and that we ourselves are not enough." Positive expectancy will attract to us positive life results. Plato said, "A grateful mind is a great mind which eventually attracts to itself great things." These great things include all that you dream and desire in life.

Oprah Winfrey states, "The more you praise and celebrate your life, the more there is in life to celebrate."

This positive approach to life is demonstrated also through a person's personality. A magnetic personality attracts friendships that we can again give thanks for.

A practice that I would recommend helping you to create a habit of giving thanks, while realizing things to be thankful for, is to write down five things you were grateful for at the end of each day.

Some will be repeated at times, and this is alright. You will be surprised at how much you are thankful for. This also helps you to focus on the positive happening s of the day instead of that which was not so great.

By programming your conscious mind to recognize and be thankful for all greatness that you enjoy in life, these then are acted upon by your subconscious and subliminal mind, then these and similar happenings manifest in your life. Again, this is the law of cause and effect.

Summary Questions
Chapter 10-Thanksgiving

Name 5 things you would like to be thankful for:

1.
2.
3.
4.
5.

Name 10 things you are thankful for:

1.
2.
3.
4.
5.
6.
7.
8.
9.
10.

Chapter 11
Service to Others in Need

The previous chapters have been about you and how to become the best possible you. You have learned to use your creative mind and to create habits that lead to your success. You have discovered how to change your life by changing your thinking, as well as how you see and attain your life's wants and needs. You have gained knowledge in the importance of being thankful, and how to forgive yourself and others.

Your personality has become positive and you are meeting new and more dynamic people. You have built your self-confidence and are stepping out of your comfort zone and trying and learning new life expanding things.

You are now ready to take your talents and abilities toward helping those in need. Mahatma Gandhi said, "We do not own the talents that we possess. We are trustees of the talent. It means we should be willing to use our talents, to help others as much as we use them for our own ambitions. We should do this not by pity, but by compassion."
It seems the world is divided between those who have plenty and those who have little or nothing. It is only when we bridge the gap through service to others that peace can be achieved, and tensions can be eliminated.

The Dalai Lama says, "If you want others to be happy, practice compassion, if you want to be happy, practice compassion." Our deepest calling is to bring love and compassion to all and the world. We are here to serve each other, to love one another and to help each other. A great way to do this is through a service club or organizations that help those in need. To join most service clubs such as: Lions, Kiwanis, Rotary, Soroptimist, and Shriners, you must be invited and sponsored by a member of the club. This is easy because you possess the attributes they are looking for. Just show interest in knowing more about their club and what they do within the community and possibly internationally and you will certainly be invited to join.

There are a multitude of nonprofit organizations that help those in need and can always use your volunteered assistance. They may be international, national, state, county or local. They are always in need of well-organized and generous people.

There are fraternal clubs that are more socially oriented, but also contribute to their community in service and fund raising.

If you served in the armed forces, there are leagues and even motorcycle clubs that help their own, and raise money to help many types of causes, such as; The American Legion and the Marine League.

You will find it exciting to be with like-minded people that share your interests. The members are always there to support you and you can call on them for assistance.

No matter if you join an organization or not, be the light of service by smiling at each person you encounter. Smiling is a great act of service.

By being of service to others, you are gaining knowledge and developing empathy toward others and it will bring you fulfillment that is healthy, energetic and heartwarming and can build self-esteem.

Summary Questions
Chapter 11-Service to Others

1.If I choose to join one of the organizations, which interests me the most?

2.Would this meet one or more of my needs? If so what need or needs.

3.If I am currently in an organization, can I contribute more in time or money?

4.If I'm not one that wishes to join a club or organization, how can I contribute my time, talents and abilities in other ways?

Chapter 12
Selective Giving

There are two types of selective giving. One is financial support to others in need either directly or to an organization that supports such needs (which could include the organizations listed in the previous chapter). The other is giving financially back (tithing) to our Source, God. That source can be nourishment to our mind body and soul. It can be giving thanks for our health and our financial wellbeing or for our church family and friends.

You may choose to contribute to a nonprofit organization that does not require your direct participation, but directly supports community needs or other needs. The principle behind this form of selective giving is to share a part of your wealth and good fortune with those less fortunate. This may also include giving back to the community that has greatly supported your business, or the organization that assisted you in time of need. Some contribute to the college they graduated from, so others can also receive an education.

Through this type of selective giving you gain personal fulfillment, through sharing with others. The social rewards of the organizations are substantial and rewarding and may even be fun.

Now let's look at tithing. Tithing means giving back to God one-tenth of everything you receive. If God is all there is, and is the creator of all, this must also include our financial source. We say, "thank you" and give a gift of appreciation to someone who has been very generous with us. Why not with God and church?

The scriptures say, 'Ask and you shall receive." This is of all good in life, not only money. Your subliminal mind, (God's mind) must have received from your conscious and thinking mind, positive thoughts, including that you are deserving and worthy of these gifts. The law of attraction is, what you think and truly believe will manifest.

You may be thinking that it is impossible at this time to tithe 10% of all that you earn. If you just start to tithe what you feel comfortable with, creating the habit of giving, is a great start. It must be done in a consciousness of total release, while understanding that the money given will not be creating a financial lack in your life.

When the Law of Attraction is activated, it begins with the conscious desire to increase your wellbeing with positive expectancy. The subliminal mind accepts this as an instruction, and it becomes manifested. When tithing, you must know that the 10% rule is proven to improve your well-being. Keep an open mind that it will work for you.

The way you receive money is really from the source of all that is, namely the highest power – God. Therefore, your source of money is neither from your paycheck, job, savings, IRA, or your pension fund. All these are channels through which money and financial resources come to you. Also, there are unexpected ways your source provides for you: a greater return from your income tax than you expected, bills that are smaller than expected, discounts on sale items that you intended to purchase, gifts or the unexpected blessings of a check in the mail. Remember, we live in an abundant and lavish universe that will provide all that we need, and it comes to us in many forms.

If you want to better understand how the law of attraction works, and how tithing can work for you, I recommend that you read the book by Edwene Gaines, "The Four Spiritual Laws of Prosperity." The first spiritual law is: you must tithe ten percent of all that you receive to the person, place or institution where you have received your spiritual food. The second law is goal setting, which I present in part 3 of this book. The third law is forgiveness, which I have already covered in part 2, chapter 4. The fourth is Divine purpose. In her book she demonstrates through her personal example how tithing has worked in her life.

The spiritual law of circulation teaches us that we can never out give God. What we give returns to us multiplied. One simple way to ignite the flow of giving and receiving in your life is to "pay it forward" in every way, including financial.

Summary Questions
Chapter 12-Selective Giving

1.Is there an organization or entity I would like to pay back financially?

2.Do I understand tithing and the principles it works on?

3. If I answered no to #2, do I feel that I should?

4. What can I do to better understand the importance of tithing?

Chapter 13
Goal Setting

If your "Recipe for Life" is to serve its purpose in bringing you your life desires and with greater results, it must be accompanied by a tangible, practical, workable plan that will give you direction and motivate you to action. Your "plan of action" puts your theories into practice, turns knowledge into know how, and thought into action. It will motivate you to a greater utilization of your full potential. You will become more time efficient, make fewer mistakes, because you know where you are headed and what you want to accomplish in your life. I was able to accomplish so much more in my life because I practice goal setting.

When you recognize the plan of action as your plan, you will begin to sense the power of your own talents, abilities and capacity to change. You will begin to come out from underneath hindering circumstances and establish a success direction. When you spend even one hour a week on your plan, it will be more than most are willing to do. In fact, it can easily put you in the top ten percent of those striving for success. It will give you that slight edge over others when applying for a job, job advancement, becoming a great athlete, or achieving personal goals.

Most people spend more time planning their vacations than planning their lives. They plan where they wish to go, how they are getting there, and they make reservations in advance for accommodations. They decide what to pack, how much money they need to put aside, what time of the year is best for that location, put in for vacation time, what sights they are going to visit, what travel agency would be best and many other planning necessities.

The vacation will turn out fine because most everything was planned with great thought, with details well outlined. Why not plan your life in the same successful way? I recommend that planning your life is even more important than planning vacations. You will use the same planning techniques that you used to crystallize your thinking and vividly visualizing where you were going and how you were getting there, and what was necessary to make it work.

Life is so much more exciting when you have a vision and you focus on where you are going and what you are creating and how and when you are getting there. For example, I wanted to learn to play tennis. To achieve this, I had to practice at least two hours per day. The next step was to enter local tournaments and I began winning some. Practice and playing in tournaments and being recognized in the newspaper, gained me recognition and I was asked to teach tennis for the city's recreation department at age fourteen.

My vision of myself as a tennis player built my confidence and desire to continue daily practice. As I entered high school and played number one position on the varsity tennis team, playing tennis became even more exiting. I rarely lost a high school tennis match and I was becoming well known socially which opened avenues that were fun to participate in. These included clubs, community and school events. The goal to become a talented tennis player continued and resulted in being in the top one percent of all the California players in the eighteen and under division. My setting short ranged goals leading to the long-ranged goal of being one of the best paid off.

The goal setting process will help you visualize possibilities that may be life changing and to use your creativity and imagination. These are key factors to accomplishments in your life. Your imagination and your ability to visualize are powerful ways to increase your intelligence and support you in bringing about feelings of peace. When you apply the power of visualization, guided imagery and your imagination, you are accessing and then harnessing the manifesting and success-seeking part of your brain. This gives you the road map to find your desired destinations. You can use the power of imagination and visualization to reach any goal and experience the life of your dreams. Visualization also reduces anxiety, stress and pain, increases energy and vitality. It promotes quality sleep and healthier management of many chronic conditions. It improves overall health and well-being.

Goal setting is a powerful technique in organizing your wants, getting you from where you are today to where you want to go, with the least effort, time and money. You will make fewer mistakes, and your decisions will be more accurate, reliable and the direction to take more visible. The deadline that you will set for reaching each goal, will produce urgency and follow through. At any time, you can measure your progress and make possible adjustments if necessary.

You may know people that are goal setters or have seen what goal setting has done for others. All athletes have set goals to become great at their chosen sport. It could have been to break the school record, gain recognition from classmates or receive an Olympic medal. The acclaimed actor practiced becoming a great actor, choosing a particular role or roles. The astronaut wanting to go to the moon had to first become an outstanding pilot and be in great physical shape. The business person, scientist, teacher, policeman, military professional and others all set goals to become the best that they could be.

Let me use an analogy of what goal setting can do for you. Picture a lake that is full of your potential including your wants and desires, your life. Your life is moving slowly toward the dam and toward the river beyond. There are many currents moving toward the dam, and the waters of your life can take many paths, around rocks, islands and channels. My point is, your life can go in many directions, and moves very slowly, unguided with little direction or planning.

On the other hand, when you set goals and you plan the basic steps to achieve them, your life now progresses and moves forward in a unidirectional pathway. Your life and desires move forward with much greater speed and forward movement. This analogy is, when your life is channeled like the river, your life moves forward with greater speed and advances in your desired direction

Summary Questions
Chapter 13-Goal Setting

1. Who do you know that is a true goal setter?

2. How has it contributed to their success?

3. Would goal setting assist you in realizing your full potential?

4. How have you used goal setting in your life?

5.Did goal setting assist you in attaining your heart's desire?

6.What advantages do you see in your becoming a greater goal setter?

7. Have you entered at least 10 wants, desires or personal changes on "My Bucket List"?

Part 3
The Application of Goal Setting

Chapter 14
Types of Goals

One type of goal is a long term-goal. It is very specific and represents the finished or ultimate achievement desired within one or more of the six areas of your life. When establishing these major goals, stretch your imagination and challenge yourself. Most of these goals will take at least 6 months and most will take one or more years to achieve, and each must have a desired date of completion.

Most people never get started and will never attain their desired goal, because they feel it is such a large undertaking and it will take too long to reach. To move forward, you need to be able to vividly see yourself reaching the goal and how it feels.

The second type of goal is a short-term goal that might be attained in one or more simple steps and can be met within 6 months. It also represents the necessary steps or goals toward a major or long-term goal. It also represents one or more progressive "victory" steps that builds your confidence of "I can" as you achieve each. This enables you to move forward toward your long-term goals. The short-term goals are a pathway to achieving the long-term goals. Short-term goals enable you to assure your progress, and these also have a deadline to their accomplishment. The realistic deadline will put urgency in achieving that step or goal. A short-term goal may lead to several long-term goals.

Some goals are called tangible. They are concrete or material things you want such as cars, boats, bicycles, a new job or promotion. They can be placed in long or short-term goals.

Intangible goals are personality developments or traits that make up your character. Many times, it takes personal development to achieve your desires or goals. These include your developing a magnetic personality, punctuality, building a positive attitude and success consciousness. These are helpful or necessary for you to achieve your major life expanding goals.

While setting a goal, you may encounter unexpected road blocks and obstacles. This is not the time to abandon your goal. You simply establish another goal that will overcome them. It may mean a slight change of plans and possibly an adjustment to your original deadline to attain your goal.

Remember, whatever you vividly imagine, ardently desire, sincerely believe, and enthusiastically act upon must inevitably become yours.

Chapter 15
Procedures/Bucket List

Now that you have completed all of the preceding chapters, you are ready to take a journey toward your desired future. The results are going to be exciting and it will be fun to see how well you have advanced in your way of thinking and your approach to your life.

If you are married or have someone that you are sharing life with, you might ask if you should fill out separate plans of action. My answer is, it is up to you. I would definitely recommend that you both work together on your action plans that relate to both of your future desires. This will ensure your lives will follow a unified direction. Isn't this why you are together? If you find togetherness has become a real-life challenge, I would recommend working on the goals program together. This has saved many marriages by helping each partner understand the needs and desires of the other.

I have found that many people have trouble beginning the goal setting process. May I suggest that you start by filling in your wants and desires and possible changes you wish to make in your life on "My Bucket List" form found in Part 4.

Enter all that would be great and exciting for you to accomplish. I recommend not filling in the forms found in the book and use the blank forms in the Part 4. Prior to filling in the form, copy several additional ones, thus keeping the originals for future use. You will notice the forms in Part 3 have been partially filled in as examples to clarify the steps and procedures of goal setting.

Keep paper and pen with you, including at your bed side, and write down all exciting ideas, thoughts and desires as they come to mind day or night. Don't let "buts" discourage you; it would be great but.... Later, when you begin analyzing your wants and desires while filling out your goals in the six areas of your life, you will have a starting point. These areas are designated as: A, B, C, D, E and F.

To further assist you in discovering additional wants, desires or self-improvements, you may wish to return to the "Chapter Review" questions and your answers at the end of each chapter in "Part 2".

Following the "Bucket List" page in the book, you will find two pages of questions to help you discover additional goals. You may find them helpful when you fill out your Bucket List and/or filling in the forms called the "Six Areas of Your Life". The simplest way to use these questions is to read them while filling in each area of your life forms. Some questions will be relevant to some of the areas and some may not. The answers for positive areas will be placed in the upper portion of each form, the answers for negative questions will be placed in the bottom portion of each.

If you have some difficulty in determining whether your desire or need you are considering is worthy to be placed as a goal, I have included the "Decision Making Process" (DMP). You may also use this form to make immediate or short term decisions. You will find the form in "Part 4". While filling in the form, you must be honest as you write the why and why-nots and as you give each a 1,2 or 3 weight of importance. When you add each column, the highest one is generally your answer or decision. I believe the rest is self-explanatory.

Remember to follow through with my recommended procedures of goal setting so this list will be acted upon and not fall to the way side as most New Year resolutions do.   Goal setting should not be frustrating or made difficult.   It should be fun and rewarding.   Once you get started, goal setting will become natural through practice. Following the "Bucket List" page, you will find five pages of questions to help you determine your goals.   You may find them helpful when filling out your Bucket List of wants and desires. These questions are to produce thoughts, ideas and goals that you enter on the forms called the "Six areas of your Life."   Also review the questions and your answers found at the end of some chapters.   Stop here and spend some time on your Bucket List in your workbook found in Part 4.

My Bucket List
Of To do's, to have, to improve my life
(keep at bedside/write down the ideas as they present themselves)

DATE	SOMETHING OBSERVED, A THOUGHT OR IDEA
3/10/19	EXAMPLE
3/10/19	Lose 20 lbs.
3/10/19	Power/fishing boat
4/10/19	Hire a yard care person
4/10/19	Increase # of friends

Questions to Promote
Ideas/Goals-Positive Areas of Life

1. What would you do if you knew you could not fail?
2. If you could snap your fingers and have anything, what would it/they be?
3. What would you really like to do?
4. What or who would you like to become?
5. What makes you feel good/about yourself?
6. What do you like/gives you pleasure?
7. What do you do that places you ahead of others?
8. What great accomplishment/s are you proud of?
9. What makes you laugh with joy?
10. What gives you the strength, energy and enthusiasm to get out of bed in the morning?
11. What motivates you?
12. What gives you a positive attitude and a great personality?
13. What will contribute to your personal growth?
14. What activities give you great pleasure?
15. What do you do that is the best use of your time?
16. When you listen to your heart, what does it tell you?
17. Are you happy in your current profession? Why or why not?
18. What avenue would you like to pursue as a career?
19. Can you see yourself as: self-employed, foreman, teacher, fireman, police-officer, Military, or...?

20. Your intuition tells you…?
21. You are grateful for…?
22. What must you do to ensure a healthy life?
23. What must you do to feel spiritually fulfilled?
24. What must you do to ensure your family is happy, secure and taken care of?
25. What is the one change you can make that would improve your life?
26. What is the one change you can make that would help others?
27. In what ways; by whom; by what, have you been inspired?
28. How can you become a great influence to others?
29. What health food do you like?
30. How can you show more empathy, love and demonstrate a magnetic personality?
31. How can you be of service to others, including those you work with?
32. How can you forgive yourself/others?
33. How can you grow more closely to nature/others?
34. My bucket list of desires should include?
35. Should you change the way you think/picture your life? If so, what should change?
36. Are you happy in this area of your life? Why?
37. You would feel more fulfilled concerning your life if…?
38. When you look back, how will you know you have truly lived your life successfully?

39. If you had the opportunity to get a message to an individual or a group, what would it be?

Questions to Promote Ideas- Negative Areas of Life

1. What would you change, if you knew you could not fail?
2. What makes you feel bad/that irritates you?
3. What do you dislike about yourself/or others?
4. What actions or thoughts make you feel inferior?
5. What actions or thoughts are you ashamed of?
6. What makes you angry or disgruntled?
7. From what or why do you not feel energetic?
8. What contributes to your sometimes negative attitude?
9. What holds you back from pursuing personal goals?
10. What activities do not give you personal pleasure?
11. What do you do that is not time effective?
12. When you look in the mirror, what do you see that you dislike?
13. Are you happy in your job? If not, why not? Is change necessary?
14. Your intuition tells you to change what?
15. Are you happy with yourself, your actions, or your thoughts? What needs to change?
16. Are you secure in this area of your life? If not what changes should you make?
17. What is holding you back? Could it be attitude, energy or thoughts?

18. Some dislike me because…What must you change?
19. Who or what type of people do you not want to associate with? Why?
20. What do others say you should change/say behind your back? What should change?
21. I need to change in this area of my life because?
22. Do you need to forgive yourself/or others? Why?
23. What negative aspects of your life need changing?
24. Upon your death, what would you change to leave a better legacy?

Chapter 16
Six Areas-Work Forms

You are now ready to go to the forms headed "Areas of Your Life." There are twelve of these pages. To get started, enter from your bucket list of wants and desires and place each in the area or areas that the goals fall under. It is possible that one goal may fall under several or possibly all of them, and most will be entered on the positive page. Place your goals that begin with a positive statement such as I will lose five pounds, I will get to know my neighbors, or single items such as a boat, or a new home.

The negative is for actions, habits or past mistakes that you feel are holding you back in life and you want to ensure they will not continue. A few examples include: I feel insecure in my job; I don't have enough money; I feel unloved; my family is dysfunctional, or I need more time. To help you recognize negatives in your life, go to "Questions to Promote Ideas/Negative Areas of Life" again. Only consider those that are of utmost concern. You want to focus on the positive aspects that will enhance your life. Most past mistakes, poor choices or upsets are of the past and should remain there.

Remember, a goal may be placed in more than one of the areas. For example, I will see life in a more positive manner (positive mental attitude). This could be advantageous in Family, Social, Mental, Spiritual and Financial areas. Another example, in Family area you may have listed a power boat to vacation with. While considering the other five, you determine it will also meet requirements in your Physical through water sports, your Mental by escaping from every day routines and relaxing on a beach and reading a book etc., Socially, you may want to expand your circle of friends by inviting them to join you fishing or boating, Spiritual by escaping to a quiet place and enjoy nature, the universe or enable you to go deep within and expand your conscious. If you own a business or have customers or clients or you have a boss, you could invite them to go with you, each could bring Financial rewards.

After you fill in the items from your bucket list, then begin adding to your Physical area first. It is generally easiest to visualize and to establish goals in. I would recommend working on your Financial goals last. There are at least two reasons for this.

1. I know through my and other's experiences that if you feel comfortable and successful in your achievements in the other five areas, and your personal growth has been taking place, your financial well-being will almost become automatic. Your self-confidence and determination will attract good in your life, including financial comfort. For example; your personal growth could bring you a raise in pay and/or promotions.

2. You may discover in order to accomplish your goals in the other five areas, it may require more income than first realized. This is not the time to go back and change or eliminate goals. It is the time to establish goals that will bring additional financial rewards. It may

require that you return to college and take one or more classes, or acquiring a college diploma, learning a trade that pays more, paying off your credit card and then paying the balance off each month, saving a lot of interest which is like getting a raise.

While setting goals, remember, do not limit your desires due to lack of money or financial needs. Do not let "buts" limit your desires such as: I would have much greater success but…, my parents did not believe…, my friends do not think…, possessions and money are evil, I do not deserve…. Let no excuses prohibit the pursuit of your desire. Remember, you have learned to overcome or avoid "blockers" within the previous chapters. You must also recall that your mind cannot conceive of an idea or want that you are not capable of achieving.

Continue filling your goals in the Six Areas of Your Life. Write two to ten in each area of your life, in the positive section and several in the negative section. Take several days if necessary, but don't procrastinate, and forget to continue the process. Continue to add to your goals as time permits. Each day can bring new ideas to you, and can present new possibilities for you to consider.

To further your knowledge of goal setting ideas and procedures, continue reading chapters 17-19 and the epilogue. Continue adding your desires and goals in the appropriate areas of your life as they come to mind in your workbook.

Sample Forms

Physical Area of My Life - A

DATE	POSITIVE GOALS
Sample Date	Sample Goal
4/24/19	Lose 20lbs.
4/24/19	Power/Fishing Boat
4/24/19	Hire a yard care person
4/24/19	Strengthen and protect my back

DATE	CURRENT NEGATIVES
Sample Date	Sample Negative
3/6/19	I am a smoker
3/6/19	I am 30lbs Overweight
3/6/19	I don't have energy
3/6/2019	My eyesight is failing

Mental Area of My Life-B

DATE	POSITIVE GOALS
Sample Date	Sample Goal
4/24/19	Increase name retention

DATE	CURRENT NEGATIVES
Sample Date	Sample Negative
3/6/19	I see life challenges as negative events
3/6/2019	I don't read enough
3/6/19	I hold grudges
3/6/19	I don't see the best in people

Social Area of My Life-C

DATE	POSITIVE GOALS
Sample Date	Sample Goal
3/17/19	Increase # of friends

DATE	CURRENT NEGATIVES
Sample Date	Sample Negative
3/17/19	I hold grudges, I don't see the best in people

Spiritual Area of My Life-D

DATE	POSITIVE GOALS
Sample Date	Sample Goal
3/10/19	Take 2 church classes per year

DATE	CURRENT NEGATIVES
Sample Date	Sample Negative
3/10/19	Church is for others; not for me

Family Area of My Life-E

DATE	POSITIVE GOALS
Sample Date	Sample Goal
3/10/19	Visit/phone each family member 2 times / yr.

DATE	CURRENT NEGATIVES
Sample Date	Sample Negative
3/10/19	Some family members hurt my feelings

Financial Area of My Life-F

DATE	POSITIVE GOALS
Sample Date	Sample Goal
4/10/19	Invest $15,000 from savings account

DATE	CURRENT NEGATIVES
Sample Date	Sample Negative
4/10/19	Money is hard for me to acquire

Chapter 17
Change Negatives to Positives

You have expressed your wants and desires in the Six Areas of Your Life.   There are several more steps to be taken while you are in this section.

First, you must decide what negatives of each area are really worth overcoming; that are really of concern and inhibiting your life or holding you back. These must be restated and become positive goals. Leaving them as they are will only reinforce the negative aspects in your life.

Here are some examples, and how to restate them as a positive goal. 1-I have trouble making friends, to, I make friends easily (long-term social goal) through (short-term goals), I will smile at people, I will complement people on their attire, walk, hair style, motivation etc., I will look for the best in people. 2-I am always sick, to, I am healthy (long-term physical goal) through (short-term goals), I will exercise for 10 minutes each day, I will drink 8 glasses of water each day, I will eat only healthy foods, I will get at least 8 hours of sleep each night. 3-I have trouble being on time, to, I am always on time (long term-social, family, mental and financial goals) through (short-term goals and include them in each area of life). I will always be on time by setting my clocks ahead by five minutes, I will include travel time. 4-I am easily frustrated to, I am calm and relaxed (long-term physical, mental, social, spiritual, family and financial goals) through (short-term goals) I will find the lesson to be learned by each event, I will breath in relaxation and exhale anxieties, I will seek professional help.

Second, the restated positive goals will be placed in the long-term or the short-term goal work sheets found in the workbook with the other positive goals found within your six areas.

You may find it advantageous to review "Part 3 – Chapter 14 "Types of Goals" before proceeding to the next chapter.

Chapter 18
Long-Term and Major Goals

Open your work book to the worksheet "Long-Term and Major Goals". Place each goal from your work sheets A, B, C, D, E, F (six areas) on the "Long-Term and Major Goals" pages, beginning on line one (see sample page of Long-Term and Major Goals). Continue placing each goal on the next numbered line. There is no order to be followed, but you may wish to place the ones that you feel are most desirable first.

On the top of the work sheet you will find the six areas listed with corresponding letters. Using the corresponding letters, place them in the column "areas satisfied" that the goal will satisfy. I have given samples of this technique on the following page. Many goals that you established in one area of your life may apply to several others as demonstrated in chapter 16 paragraph 3. Leave the short-term goals necessary column open at this time. The date accomplished column will become your final entry when you achieve the goal.

Most of the goals found on this form will be broken down into several smaller goals or steps making them more measurable and to build your self-confidence and determination as you attain each.

Keep this work sheet available; you are now ready to fill in the short-term goals work sheet.

Long Term and Major Goals

Physical (A) Social (B) Mental (C) Spiritual (D) Family (E) Financial (F)

Date Entered	Goal #	Goals	Area(s) Satisfied	Short Term Steps	Date Met
3/6/19	1	Lose 20 lbs.	ABCEF	1,2	
3/10/19	2	Power/fishing boat	ABCDEF	3,4,5,12,13	
3/17/19	3	Hire a yard care person	ABE	5,12,13	
3/17/19	4	Increase # of friends	BC	1,2,3,4,6,7,8,9,12,13	
3/10/19	5	Take 2 church classes / yr	BCD	9,10	
3/10/19	6	Visit or ph. ea. family member 2+times / yr.	BCE	9,10,11	
3/17/19	8	I have a strong back	ACEF	1,2,5	
4/10/19	7	Invest $15000 from savings account	BEF	11,12	
4/10/19	8	I will read 1 book/month	BCDEF	6,12,14	
4/11/19	9	I will understand & practice forgiveness	BCDE	6,7,15,16	
4/11/19	10	Eye Care	ABEF	17	

Chapter 19
Short-Term Goals

While you examine your list of "Long-Term Goals" work sheet, you realize that many of the goals will take some time and effort. This is why they are long- term goals and may take six months, a year or more to achieve. You must take one step at a time. Short-term goals do just that.

Open your work book to "Short-Term Goals, Steps and Deadlines" and with your Long-Term goals in hand, consider the first one. Ask what steps or tasks must I perform to achieve that long-term goal? Place each of the short-term goals or steps that apply on a numbered line or goal on the work sheet. (See sample worksheet on of Short-Term Goals.) Try also to determine what obstacles or road blocks you may encounter and present them as necessary steps or goals or solutions to be taken. The road blocks and obstacles will become short-term goals that will overcome the foreseen hurdle.

When you determine that you have listed all steps necessary to accomplish that goal, enter each number on the corresponding line on the long-term goal in the "short-term goals" column that would be a step toward its attainment (see samples on previous page). Go to the next long term goal and follow suit.

Many short-term goals may be steps or goals that will pertain to other long-term goals. Upon entering each new long-term goal, review all preceding short-term goals to see if they may apply to that particular goal. You will see that many may apply. Place all short-term goals and corresponding numbers pertaining to that goal in mentioned column. Continue this procedure until you have completed the goals found on the long-term goal work sheet.

Now give a realistic deadline to all of the short-term goals and place the date in the target date column. In reviewing the target dates of all short-term goals that apply to the long-termed goal, you can anticipate the completion date of the long-term goal.

To help you pick out the most valuable goals that you wish to get started on, review the "areas satisfied column ". The goals that have the greatest number of letters will generally be of priority. You might say they will give you the greatest "Bang for the Bucks". Start accomplishing the necessary steps to their achievement. The goals that are in the "short-term goals necessary" column should be considered in two ways:

First, the goals that have the most steps are probably the goals that may take the longest time to achieve. Is it worth the time and effort? If so get started now.

Second, the goals with the least necessary steps or numbers will generally be easier to accomplish and in the shortest time.

You should choose a mixture of the easiest, the more difficult as well as the goals you feel are the most important to you. If you choose only the easiest ones first, it is like a project list, leaving the more difficult ones last and never "having enough time, energy or money" to get them under way or they fall to the wayside.

Upon the completion of all the short-term goals that apply to a long-term goal, you should have arrived at your desired goal. Congratulate yourself in a meaningful way for a job well done.

When you complete the long-term and the shot-term goal work sheets, you have all you need to prioritize and plan your pathway to achieve your greater success.

Continue reviewing your goals weekly to keep on course and to let your minds (subconscious and subliminal) work on manifesting the goal. Ideas, solutions and intuitions will be working for you day and night.

As you work toward their completion, you are developing the habit of goal setting and the process will become more natural. As you progress, you will take on more goals from your list. It will not be long until you will realize that you need to establish more long-term goals. You may have accomplished them or some may have been revised or replaced by new desires or goals. You should review the previous goals that were not of priority. They may have become important at this time.

As you continue working your plan of action (goal setting) and accomplish goal upon goal, you are becoming the real and desirable you, while gaining self confidence in all that you choose. The confidence you have and are continuing to build will build enthusiasm and energy to establish even greater and higher goals.

When practicing goal setting, I would suggest you reinforce your ability as a goal setter by posting the following affirmation: I AM A MASTER GOAL SETTER! Make up other affirmations that you wish to remind yourself to be mindful of. Place them on the refrigerator, on a wall or on your dressing mirror. It is a great reminder to you and also to your subconscious mind.

In the workbook I have posted some of my "Affirmations and Daily Reminders" that you may wish to post in various locations.

Short Term Goals, Steps and Deadlines

#	Goal	Target Date
1	Exercise on exercise bike 10 min./day	3/20/19
2	Walk 2 mi. /day	3/20/19
3	Research boats	3/17/19
4	Save for down payment	7/10/19
5	Research yard care persons/call	4/17/19
6	Read positive materials	Continuous
7	Look at the best in people	Continuous
8	Be a good listener	Continuous
9	Place events on calendar	3/10/19
10	Schedule event for classes	3/10/19
11	Visit or phone a family member each week	3/15/19
12	Research investment interests	3/12/19
13	Schedule appt. w/investment counselor	3/16/19
14	Set aside 2 hrs/wk; 1 evening/wk to read	Continuous
15	I will read various types to expand my knowledge	Continuous
16	I will practice forgiveness	Continuous
17	I will schedule an eye exam	05/18/19

Epilogue

By this time you should realize that your life is much different from when you started "Your Recipe for Life." Positive and exiting things are now happening in your life that you had only wished for, but you did not dream could happen to you.

Please remember you are a winner and your mind is as powerful as you believe it to be, and it is even greater. Program it well and protect your thoughts, for your life depends on it. Treat others with respect and treat them as you would like them to treat you; and a smile goes a long way in making someone feel good. I know that you will not be a person that wakes up one morning and realizes that life has passed you by, as many others will. "Go Live Your Life," song writer and singer Wade Hayes states. He overcame cancer twice with less than a 15% chance for survival.

You are a master goal setter and can accomplish any desire that you wish for. You possess all the "tools of knowledge" that are necessary for you to lead the life of your dreams. You also can be a great influence to your family and friends, a very useful tool when used appropriately. You are and have been setting an example to others that surround you. They have noticed that you possess a great deal of confidence in everything you do. You are a great achiever and you look at everything in a positive and successful manner. Believe me when I say that others have noticed these great assets that you possess, and many may have expressed this to you already.

Keep up the good work. Yours in Success, *Fred*

PART 4
BLANK WORK FORMS

INCLUDING AFFIRMATIONS
& DAILY GUIDES

You may download the Blank Forms, Affirmations and Guides by going to www.yourrecipe4life.com.

YOUR RECIPE for LIFE
WORK FORMS

CONTENTS

Introduction

You are continuing your journey toward a new and exciting way of life. You will find your life being gradually, or in some cases immediately, positively transformed. The work forms have the plan of action work sheets necessary to organize all you wish to realize through your desires and goals. It will crystalize your thoughts into action.

You have been introduced or reintroduced to ideas and challenges through reading "Your Recipe for Life".

Part One was to help you realize how your mind functions and how to protect the thoughts being processed by your mind and how your mind controls your life. What you think is what you become and what manifests in your life. You must protect your thoughts by staying positive and success conscious.

Part Two presented what the author feels are the eight success essentials required for you to become the success you want and deserve.

Part Three is the application and the design of goal setting. It covered the types of goals found in the six areas of life. It helped you to choose your wants, desires and goals you wish to pursue and accomplish and how to prioritize your goals.

The work forms include all you will need to organize and plan the steps necessary to achieve your desires. As you fill in the forms, it will become evident to which goals are of priority. You will need to follow the instructions and examples found in the book.

Enclosed are affirmations and daily reminders you may wish to cut out and place in strategic places, such as on the refrigerator, mirror, dashboard, etc.; add your personal ones also. Remember, your subconscious mind will be taking them as instructions to bring your life desires into form or into manifestation.

Happy trails ,

Fred

MY BUCKET LIST
Of "To Do's", To Have, & To improve my life
(Keep close, write down thoughts).

DATE	SOMETHING OBSERVED, A THOUGHT OR IDEA

FRED'S RECIPE FOR LIFE
DECISION MAKING PLAN
SHORT FORM FOR DECISION MAKING (DMP)

Item I am considering:

_____

SCORING:
Very Important Consideration = 3 Pts.
Important Consideration = 2 Pts
Should Be Considered = 1 Pt.

WHY CHANGE/ WHY PROCEED	PTS	WHY NOT?	PTS
1			
2			
3			
4			
5			
6			
7			
8			
9			
10			
11			
GREATEST SCORE WINS			

Also consider if close, what does my heart say and what is my gut feeling; What is my highest calling?

Physical Area of My Life - A

DATE	POSITIVE GOALS

DATE	CURRENT NEGATIVES

Mental Area of My Life-B

DATE	POSITIVE GOALS

DATE	CURRENT NEGATIVES

Social Area of My Life-C

DATE	POSITIVE GOALS

DATE	CURRENT NEGATIVES

Spiritual Area of My Life-D

DATE	POSITIVE GOALS

DATE	CURRENT NEGATIVES

Family Area of My Life-E

DATE	POSITIVE GOALS

DATE	CURRENT NEGATIVES

Financial Area of My Life-F

DATE	POSITIVE GOALS

DATE	CURRENT NEGATIVES

Long Term and Major Goals

Physical (A) Social (B) Mental (C) Spiritual (D) Family (E) Financial (F)

Date Entered	Goal #	Goals	Area(s) Satisfied	Short Term Steps	Date Met

Short-Term Goals, Steps and Deadlines

#	Goal	Target Date
1		
2		
3		
4		
5		
6		
7		
8		
9		
10		
11		
12		
13		
14		
15		
16		
17		
18		

AFFIRMATIONS and DAILY REMINDERS

Affirmations declare positively that something is true. An affirmation is a positive statement asserting that the goal you wish to achieve is already happening. Affirmations are effective tools for training your thoughts and feelings regarding what you desire to experience in your life.

Daily reminders are positive statements or famous quotes that remind you to keep your mind focused on the positive and the success that surrounds you daily. They are positive thoughts or statements and reminders to see only good surrounding and within you.

The following pages are affirmations and daily reminders you may want to cut out and place on your closet door, mirror, walls, lamp shades, refrigerator door, car dash or on the ceiling over your bed. Some of the affirmations and daily reminders may not seem relevant while others may. Use the ones that are meaningful to you. Add to them when you discover ones you feel will assist you. They will create the habit of thought or way of thinking that will bring successful manifestations to you. They are positive instructions to your subliminal or subconscious mind. Your mind will subconsciously steer and guide you both day and night. These thoughts will help you to recognize the greatness and the abundance within you and your surroundings.

I will leave you with a few last thoughts:

Nothing is more powerful than an idea whose time has come.

Your mind is the most powerful, transformative tool you have.

All change comes from within you and begins in mind.

Your mind will work for you or against you in direct accordance to what you believe and think.

Once you decide to use your mind for good, you become stronger and more capable of achieving your wants and desires than ever before. Now is the time to live your life's dreams.

Travel well-Positive Expectancy,

Fred

AFFIRMATIONS

LIKES ATTRACTS LIKE. I CHOSE MY THOUGHTS AND FRIENDS WELL.

LIFE IS NOT A DRESS REHEARSAL. I LIVE IN THE NOW, LIVE WELL, SHOW EXCITEMENT. I MAKE EACH MINUTE COUNT.

I ONLY THINK OF SUCCESS. SUCCESS CONSCIOUSNESS PRODUCE IDEAS THAT PRODUCE SUCCESS

I HAVE WHAT IT TAKES TO ACCOMPLISH WHAT I DESIRE.

I SHOW GREAT INTEREST IN THE PERSON I AM TALKING WITH BEFORE I TELL THEM ABOUT ME.

MY LIFE IS EXCITING AND GREAT.

I CHANGE MY THINKING WHICH CHANGES MY LIFE. POSITIVE THOUGHTS BRINGS FORTH GOOD AND GREAT RESULTS.

I STOP BEING WHO I WAS AND I CHANGE INTO WHO I AM.

I AM ONE WITH ALL CREATION. I LOOK AT THE WONDERS SURROUNDING ME; THE SKY, TREES, LAKES, BIRDS, FLOWERS PEOPLE, MOM, DAD, GRANDMA ECT.

I APPRECIATE AND GIVE THANKS OFTEN FOR THESE SURROUNDING BEAUTIES.

TRUST WILL BE BUILT OVER TIME WHEN I CONTINUALLY AM CONSISTENTLY RELIABLE AND ALIGNED WITH TRUTH IN MY WORDS AND ACTIONS.

THIS DAY, I LISTEN TO AND HONOR MY INNERMOST VOICE. I CHOOSE TO LIVE FROM MY HEART. I AM MOST ALIGNED WITH MY HEART WHEN I AM GENEROUS.

I TAKE TIME TO RECOGNIZE AND TO GIVE THANKS FOR ALL THE GOOD THAT IS.

MY MIND IS THE MOST POWERFUL TRANSFORMATIONAL TOOL I POSSES. I PROGRAM IT WITH CARE.

MY SUCCESS IS WITHIN; I BUILD MY "TOOLS OF KNOWLEDGE" WHICH HELPS ME AND OTHERS.

I LOVE, LAUGH, LIVE LIFE. IT IS HEALTHY AND WISE.

I LOOK FOR THE BEST IN PEOPLE EVEN THOUGH THEY MAY THINK, ACT OR DO THINGS DIFFERENTLY THAN I DO.

GOD IS LOVE AND ALL THERE IS. I AM GOD IN EXPRESSION THEREFOR I AM LOVE. DEMONSTRATE LOVE AND APPRECIATE IT ALWAYS.

I LIVE AND ACT AS A CHILD- UNINHIBITED AND JOYFUL. WHAT I DO AND THINK IS WHAT COUNTS.

I HAVE A GREAT AND DYNAMIC PERSONALITY

I SPEAK MY WORD FOR THE HIGHEST AND THE BEST FOR MYSELF AND OTHERS.

I SPEAK AND ACT WITH INTEGRITY.

I USE MY IMAGINATION AND I AM CREATING A LIFE OF LOVE AND JOY.

I CREATE AND IMAGINE A LIFE FULL OF UNLIMITED POTENTIAL.

PROJECT MY VOICE WITH ENTHUSIASM AND CONFIDENCE.

I CHOOSE TO BE ACCOUNTABLE FOR MY LIFE.

MY HEART REJOICES IN THE REALITY OF FREEDOM TO EXPRESS ALL THAT I AM.

I ACCEPT THEM WITH A GRATEFUL HEART.

I IMAGINE EACH DAY WITH A NEW OUTLOOK ON LIFE; AN ALL-ENCOMPASSING VISION, A DEEPER REALIZATION.

I AM USING MY IMAGINATION TO CREATE A LIFE FULL OF JOY, FUN, HARMONY, BALANCE AND GROWTH

I GIVE THANKS FOR ALL I HAVE AND THAT ALL MY NEEDS ARE BEING MET.

I AM PROSPEROUS. I AM SO BECAUSE I CHOOSE TO KNOW THAT I AM SO.

I KNOW MY CREATED GOALS ARE COMPLETE.

I REFUSE TO LISTEN TO LIES AND NEGATIVE THINKING. THEY ONLY BRING MISERY AND FAILURE.

PROSPERITY IS ALL AROUND ME. I AM OPEN TO RECEIVE IT.

POSITIVE EXPECTANCY SPEEDS PROGRESS. I LIVE IN CONTINUAL STATE OF EXPECTANCY.

I LOOK FOR AND I SEE ONLY THE GOOD IN ALL THINGS.

WHEN I AM FACED WITH A CHALLENGE, I STOP AND LISTEN TO MY INNER CALM OR INTUITION FOR THE ANSWER.

INEXHAUSTIBLE ENERGY EXISTS AT MY CENTER OF BEING.

MY IMAGINATION AND INTUITION COMES FROM THE SPIRIT THAT KNOWS ALL THINGS.

I AM GRATEFUL FOR THE FULFILLMENT OF MY DREAMS AND DESIRES.

I PLAN DAILY FOR MY LIFE DEVELOPMENTS BECAUSE LIFE IS NOT STATIC.

I AM ALWAYS FRIENDLY; THERE-FORE I ATTRACT FRIENDS EASILY.

I USE MY IMAGINATION REMEMBERING THAT WHICH I WANT BEGINS AS A THOUGHT.

I LIVE IN THE PRESENT MOMENT AND I PLAN FOR THE FUTURE.

MY LIFE IS FILLED WITH ACCEPTANCE FOR ALL PEOPLE.

I AM ALWAYS ON TIME. PEOPLE ADMIRE ME.

I HAVE WHAT I NEED TO LIVE A JOYFUL, PROSPEROUS AND LOVE FILLED LIFE.

I CHANGE MY THINKING. I CHANGE MY LIFE. I STOP LIVING FROM EFFECT TO LIVING FROM CAUSE. I AM TRUSTWORTHY AND PEOPLE HAVE CONFIDENCE IN ME.

I AM HAPPY, JOYFUL AND DEDICATED IN ALL I CHOOSE TO DO.

I AM SUCCESSFUL, ABUNDANT AND CONFIDENT.

I DEMONSTRATE INTEGRITY IN ALL I SAY AND DO.

MY LIFE IS FULL OF JOY. I CHOOSE TO BE HAPPY.

I KNOW NOTHING CAN KEEP MY GOOD FROM ME. I AM DESERVING.

I CAN CHOOSE TO BE RIGHT OR TO BE HAPPY.

I AM A GREAT _____.

I IDENTIFY MYSELF WITH SUCCESS. I AM SUCCESSFUL.

THE PLANET NEEDS A LEADER OF LOVE. I AM THE ONE TO SHOW THE WAY.

I HAVE A BEAUTIFUL AND POWERFUL BODY AND MIND.

WHEN I TAKE A WALK IN NATURE, I SEE BEAUTY, AWE AND GOD.

MY MOTIVATION AND REWARD CENTERS OF MY BRAIN ARE ACTIVATED WHEN I WILLINGLY DONATE TO CHARITY.

MY LIFE IS FILLED WITH EASE AND BEAUTY.

TODAY I FINISH WHAT I START.

I AM GRATEFUL FOR ALL THE ABUNDANCE THAT FLOWS TO ME ALWAYS.

I CHOOSE TO BE COMPASSIONATE TOWARD MYSELF AND OTHERS.

I SMILE ALWAYS; SMILES ARE CONTAGIOUS.

GOD IS ALL THERE IS IN THE ENTIRE UNIVERSE, THERE-FORE GOD IS WITHIN ME AND EXPRESSES THROUGH ME.

I SHOW LOVE TOWARD OTHERS AND IT WARMS MY HEART.

MY PETS SEND THEIR LOVE TO ME. I INTURN SEND MY LOVE TO THEM.

I EMBRACE MY HEART OF SERVICE AS I MOVE THROUGH THE ACTIVITIES OF LIFE.

I AM CONTENT AND PEACE SURROUNDS ME ALWAYS.

TRUST WILL BE BUILT OVER
TIME WHEN I
CONTINUALLY AM
CONSISTENTLY RELIABLE
AND ALIGNED WITH TRUTH

I AM LOVABLE THEREFORE
I LOVE ALL BEINGS AND
ALLOW THEM TO LOVE ME.

I DISASSOCIATE WITH ALL
THOUGHTS OF LACK.

I THINK GOOD AND
POSITIVE THOUGHTS AND I
TEND THEM REGULARLY.

I KNOW THAT I AM WHOLE
AND PERFECT TODAY AND
EVERY DAY.

HI ACE (while looking in a
mirror)

I LOVE MEETING PEOPLE.

GOD LOVES ME AND IS
WITH ME ALWAYS.

I LOVE RETIREMENT AND
USE MY TIME WISELY.

MY LIFE IS PROSPEROUS

I CAN ACCOMPLISH
ANYTHING MY HEART
DESIRES.

I THINK I CAN THEREFORE I
KNOW I CAN.

I LOVE LIFE.

I AM A FORGIVING
PERSON.

I MAKE EVERY MINUTE
COUNT, FOR IT WILL BE
GONE IN A HEART BEAT.

I LOVE NEW EXCITEMENT
AND CHALLENGES.

I AM ALWAYS POLITE
WHEN ADDRESSING
PEOPLE.

I ACT IN A PLEASING
MANNER AND PEOPLE
TAKE NOTICE.

DAILY REMINDERS

WE CANNOT LIVE A CHOICE-LESS LIFE. EVERY DAY, EVERY MOMENT, EVERY SECOND, THERE IS CHOICE. IF IT WERE NOT SO, WE WOULD NOT BE INDIVIDUALS.
-DR. ERNEST HOLMES

THOUGHT IS FIRST CAUSE AND IS PLACED IN MY MIND. EFFECT IS THE RESULT, OUTCOME OR MAGNIFICATION OF MY THOUGHT.

THE MIND CANNOT CONCEIVE THAT WHICH IS IMPOSSIBLE.

FORGIVENESS CLEARS NEGATIVE THOUGHTS SO YOU CAN SEE GOOD. REMEMBER, YOU MUST FORGIVE YOURSELF FIRST.

WHEN YOU HELP OTHERS, OTHERS WILL WANT TO HELP YOU. "PAY IT FORWARD" NOT EXPECTING AN IMMEDIATE RETURN.

GOD IS ALL THERE IS AND IS LOVE. GOD IN ME EXPRESSES LOVE AND I DEMONSTRATE IT AND APPRECIATE IT ALWAYS.

SMILES ARE CONTAGIOUS AND ARE OFTEN RETURNED.

THERE IS NO SUCH THING AS FAILURE-JUST A CHALLENGE OR LEARNING EXPERIENCE.

PERSONALITY IS THE OUTER EXPRESSION OF ONE'S INNER ATTITUDE. ALWAYS CONTINUE BUILDING A POSITIVE MENTAL ATTITUDE.

EVERYTHING THAT IS SHOWING UP IN ONES LIFE IS A DIRECT RESULT OF THEIR MENTAL PICTURE OR THOUGHT THAT THEY HAVE ABOUT THEMSELVES AND THEIR LIFE.

IDEAS PLANTED IN MIND WILL ALWAYS BECOME FORM.

EVERYTHING HAPPENS TWICE- ONCE IN YOUR MIND, THEN IN YOUR OUTER EXPERIENCE.

ABUNDANCE IS NOT SOMETHING YOU ACQUIRE, IT IS SOMETHING YOU TUNE INTO.
-DR. WAYNE DYER

THE GREATEST OF ALL REMEDIES FOR FEAR IS A BURNING DESIRE FOR ACHIEVEMENT, BACKED BY USEFUL ACTION IN PURSUIT OF YOUR AIM.
-NAPOLEON HILL

WHEN I AM CONFUSED, I STOP AND LISTEN TO MY INNER CALM.

FEARS ARE SIMPLY THOUGHT PROJECTIONS OF FALSE EVIDENCE APPEARING REAL.

THOUGHT BECOMES AN IDEA WHICH BECOMES A VISION WHICH BECOMES BELIEF. THEY SET ENERGY INTO MOTION TO MANIFEST INTO FORM.
-THE SECRET

SPIRIT IS THOUGHT. MATTER IS FORM. FORM HAS SPACE AND TIME PARAMETERS; THOUGHT HAS NEITHER.
-THOMAS TOWARD

LUCK IS PREPARATION MEETING OPPORTUNITY.
-PAUL J. MEYER

NO PROBLEM CAN BE SOLVED FROM THE SAME LEVEL OF CONSCIOUSNESS THAT CREATED IT.
- ALBERT EINSTEIN

WITHOUT EXCEPTION, THAT WHICH YOU GIVE THOUGHT TO IS THAT WHICH YOU BEGIN TO INVITE INTO YOUR EXPERIENCE.
- ESTER HICKS

FAITH- EVIDENCE OF THINGS NOT SEEN.

CONSCIOUSNESS IS AN INVISIBLE MENTAL ACTIVITY WHICH MANIFESTS ITSELF IN THE WORLD OF FORM.
- DR. DAVID ALEXANDER

WE ARE NOT HUMAN BEINGS HAVING A SPIRITUAL EXPERIENCE; WE ARE SPIRITUAL BEINGS HAVING A HUMAN EXPERIENCE.

YOUR BELIEFS BECOME YOUR THOUGHTS. YOUR THOUGHTS BECOME YOUR WORDS. YOUR WORDS BECOME YOUR ACTIONS. YOUR ACTIONS BECOME YOUR HABITS. YOUR HABITS BECOME YOUR VALUES. YOUR VALUES BECOME YOUR DESTINY.
- MAHATMA GANDHI

WE DON'T GET WHAT WE ASK FOR, WE GET WHAT WE EXPECT.
- DR. ERNEST HOLMES

NAMASTE- THE LIGHT WITHIN ME HONORS THE LIGHT WITHIN YOU.
-HINDU EXPRESSION

WE SHOULD CAREFULLY CONSIDER WHETHER WE ARE WILLING TO EXPERIENCE THE RESULTS OF OUR THOUGHTS.

REACH FOR THE DIRECTION OF WHAT YOU ARE WANTING AND FEEL THE NEW MANIFESTATION.
- ESTER HICKS

TWO GREAT PRINCIPLES- GOD IS WITHIN AND THOUGHT IS CREATIVE.
- THE LOST SYMBOL BY DAVID BROWN

A GRATEFUL MIND IS A MIND WHICH EVENTUALLY
ATTRACTS ITSELF TO GREAT THINGS.
- PLATO

WE ARE OUR OWN IMAGINERS, AND WHAT WE SEE
IS WHAT WE GET. IMAGINE THAT.
- NANCY FAGAN

THE MORE YOU PRAISE AND CELEBRATE YOUR LIFE,
THE MORE THERE IS IN LIFE TO CELEBRATE.
- OPRAH WINFREY

IT IS NOT EASY TO FIND HAPPINESS IN OURSELVES,
AND IT IS IMPOSSIBLE TO FIND IT ELSEWHERE.
- AGNES REPPLIER

WE DON'T SEE THINGS AS THEY ARE, WE SEE
THINGS AS WE ARE.
- ANAIS NIN

HIDDEN IN EVERY PROBLEM LIES AN OPPORTUNITY
SO POWERFUL THAT IT LITERALLY DWARFS THE
PROBLEM.
- ALBERT EINSTEIN

OUR BELIEFS DRIVE OUR THOUGHTS, WHICH IN
TURN DRIVE OUR ACTIONS. THE END RESULTS
SHOW UP AS THE CIRCUMSTANCE OF OUR LIVES.
- REV. JANE BEACH

GOD ALWAYS SAYS YES TO YOUR THOUGHTS AND STATEMENTS. MAKE SURE THEY ARE POSITIVE AND NOT NEGATIVE ONES

FORGIVENESS IS PERSONAL GROWTH, UNDERSTANDING AND IS DEMONSTRATED BY PERSONALITY.

IT DOESN'T MATTER HOW MUCH YOU HAVE. IT ALL MEANS NOTHING IF YOU ARE NOT HAPPY WITH YOURSELF.

WE ATTRACT WHAT WE THINK ABOUT. AS IN MIND SO IN MANIFESTATION; WHERE ATTENTION GOES, ENERGY FLOWS.

PERFECT IS GOOD. DONE IS BETTER.

YOU ARE WHERE YOU ARE TODAY THROUGH THE SUM TOTAL OF ALL YOUR PREVIOUS THOUGHTS AND BELIEFS.
-FRED TAUNTON

YOU EXPERIENCE HELL THROUGH YOUR THOUGHTS AND WRONGFUL ACTIONS.

MEDITATION BRINGS ABOUT ANSWERS, IDEAS AND INTUITIONS.

ANY PERSON WILL ATTRACT THAT TO WHICH HE OR SHE GIVES CONSISTENT ATTENTION, ENERGY AND FOCUS.

LOOK FOR AND SEE ONLY WHAT YOU WISH TO EXPERIENCE.

NEGATIVE AND LIMITING BELIEFS ARE REPETITIVE THOUGHTS, WHICH HOLD YOU BACK FROM CREATING WHAT IT IS YOU WISH TO EXPERIENCE.

BELIEFS, WHETHER THEY ARE POSITIVE OR NEGATIVE, SHAPE YOUR EXPERIENCE.

THOUGHT IS NOT ONLY POWER, IT IS ALSO THE FORM OF ALL THINGS.

THE CONDITIONS THAT WE ATTRACT WILL CORRESPOND EXACTLY TO OUR MENTAL PICTURES.

KNOW THAT NO MATTER WHAT OTHERS MAY SAY, THINK OR DO, YOU ARE A SUCCESS.

KNOW NOTHING CAN HINDER YOU FROM ACCOMPLISHING YOUR GOOD.

ALL THE POWER IN THE UNIVERSE IS WITH YOU; FEEL IT, KNOW IT, AND THEN ACT AS THOUGH IT WERE TRUE.

GENEROSITY CONSISTS NOT IN THE SUM GIVEN
BUT IN THE MANNER IN WHICH IT IS BESTOWED.

AS SOON AS YOU TRUST YOURSELF, YOU WILL
KNOW HOW TO LIVE.

WE CREATE OUR OWN REALITY THROUGH OUR
THOUGHTS AND EMOTIONS.

Some final thoughts and infamous quotations:

"Abundance is not something you acquire, it is something you tune into." - Dr. Wayne Dyer

"The greatest of all remedies for fear, is a burning desire for achievement, by useful action in pursuit of your aim."
- Napoleon Hill

"Luck is preparation meeting opportunity." - Paul J. Myers

"No Problem can be solved from the same level of consciousness that created it."-Albert Einstein

"We don't get what we ask for, we get what we expect."
-Dr. Ernest Holmes

" A grateful mind is a mind which eventually attracts itself to great things." - Plato

"It is not easy to find happiness in ourselves, and it is impossible to find it elsewhere." - Agnes Repplier

"We don't see things as they are, we see things as we are."
- Anais Nin

"Don't wake up one day to see it's passed you by - Go Live Your Life." - Wade Hayes

Made in the USA
Middletown, DE
10 September 2020